# THE PRINCIPLES OF AMERICAN PROSPERITY

By
**LEIGHTON A. WILKIE**
and
**RICHARD STANTON RIMANOCZY**

A WINONA PRESS, INC. PUBLICATION
distributed by THE DEVIN-ADAIR COMPANY
Old Greenwich, Connecticut 06870

ISBN 0-8159-6513-3
LIBRARY OF CONGRESS CATALOGUE NO. 75-7292

# HOW TO READ THIS BOOK

This book is eclectic — meaning that the reader can open it at random and find a self-contained three or four minute exposition of a pertinent thought. The expanded Table of Contents permits selection of the topics that are of most interest to the reader at any particular time. This feature and the economic dictionary make it a book to be retained and kept constantly at hand.

From earliest times, man has been groping for the best way to do the essential things needed for a successful, orderly, peaceful, and prosperous society.

Without any rule book to follow, this has been a process of trial and error in which the same mistakes have been made over and over.

The reason for this is man's failure to keep a clear cumulative record of what has been tried, what has succeeded, and what has failed. As Sir John Buchon said: "The hasty reformer who does not remember the past will find himself condemned to repeat it."

The purpose of this book is to present in simple condensed form the nature of the problem, the proven successes, and the reasons for the failures. The text simply puts the facts that must be dealt with in their proper context. The assembled facts, therefore, form principles to guide our behavior.

These principles do not care whether we observe or ignore them. But their influence over our material welfare is inescapable. When we act in consonance with them, we benefit. When we flout them, we suffer.

The simplified, non-technical language of this book makes basic economics understandable to everyone. It is the publisher's hope that it will become a permanent source of practical knowledge and wisdom for our economically confused society.

# TABLE OF CONTENTS

## Chapter II — THE EVOLUTION OF PRODUCTION

# Chapter III — THE EVOLUTION OF EXCHANGE

# Chapter IV — SOME CURRENT ECONOMIC CONSIDERATIONS

# Chapter V — UNSOLVED PROBLEMS

## Chapter VI — GLOSSARY OF ECONOMIC TERMINOLOGY

# ILLUSTRATIONS, CHARTS AND DIAGRAMS

# THE IMPORTANCE OF THINKING
## "IN THE TOTALITY"

In this book you will occasionally see the phrase: "In the totality." It is of such importance to proper understanding that this page is devoted to its meaning.

When we say: "In the totality, we get our employment from each other," the "we" means everyone gainfully employed or holding claims on goods and services (that is, money) earned in previous periods.

When we say: "In the totality, it is our purchases that provide our payroll," we mean everyone's purchases.

When we say: "In the totality, if we try to charge ourselves more than we are willing to pay, we reduce our purchases and therefore reduce employment" we are talking about the entire economy. As has been said, we make our living taking in each others' laundry.

It is easy enough for the individual, the single business or the single group to think: "What I choose to do for my benefit will have very little impact on the total economy," but they are wrong. Every economic action creates reaction. Everything in the total economy, like marbles in a glass, is interrelated with everything else. The reaction may be swift or slow, but it is inevitable.

Economic actions, especially selfish actions, are contagious. Small groups can, temporarily, take advantage of others, but the disadvantaged quickly retaliate. If everyone gets a raise, no one gets a raise, because the money will not buy any more. Only when there is an increase in productivity can there be an increase in one man's or one group's compensation without taking something away from others, either directly or through depreciation of the purchasing power of the dollar.

Every intelligent person, in his own interest, should ask himself: "What would happen to the economy, and to me, if everyone did what I am about to do?"

We know that this is asking more restraint than most people will exercise, but the extent to which they do do it will increase the prosperity of all—the welfare of the totality.

# THE NATURE
# OF MAN

1

# HOMO SAPIENS – THE ANIMAL
# LEAST LIKELY TO SUCCEED

Man is nature's latest addition to the world's fauna. Judged by animal standards he would have had to be voted the least likely to succeed in his hostile environment. He has no fur or hairy hide to protect him from the elements. He has no fangs or claws. He is a poor climber. He is slow afoot. And nature offers him very little natural ready-to-eat food.

But man has had two exclusive advantages: a hand instead of a paw or a hoof, and a tremendously superior brain. The hand, with its opposing thumb, made him the only creature that could hold and use tools for throwing, striking, pounding, scraping, turning, and twisting. The brain enabled him to recognize a natural tool when he saw it, and imagine how it could be improved.

So man, instead of having to conform to nature, was able to make nature serve his needs. He was unique in being able to learn to produce things he wanted by changing the form, condition, and place of natural things.

Man had a big problem not shared by any other creature. His brain forced him to wonder where he came from, where he was going after death, and how he was supposed to live with his fellow man. Unlike other members of the animal kingdom, he had no instinctive rule book. This was made more serious by his combative nature. Man is one of the few creatures that kills his own kind. During recorded human history, there have been almost no periods when wars were not in progress.

Yet man professes to love peace and hate war. He has a split personality that makes him love and hate many things, and his attitudes and feelings are often unpredictable and contradictory.

He loves freedom of action for himself but not always for others. He supports the need for government as a necessity for law and order, but recognizes it as his potential enemy. In his economic life he will fight for the privilege of free competition for himself but resents it when others use it too effectively. He knows that co-operation is a necessity for progress and prosperity, but frequently withholds his own when he thinks it is to his advantage.

Man's ignorance concerning the best way to live with others must be considered in the framework of time. No one knows how many millions of years it took the members of the animal kingdom to work out a society orderly enough to permit their survival. No one knows how many species are now extinct because they were unable to work it out.

Man is the "new kid on the block." He has been working at the job of developing a viable society for such a short time that, on the world's time scale, it is as if he started only yesterday. It is too soon, therefore, to say that homo sapiens will not make it, that his superior intelligence will combine with his lack of wisdom and penchant for irrational behavior to bring on his self destruction. Man's scientific progress has been breathtaking, but his lack of understanding of human relations is deeply discouraging.

Through the pertinent facts highlighted here in both of these areas, hopefully, the reader will become a wiser and more constructive member of this "experimental" society.

# YOU'VE GOT TO BE YOU

To live successfully every living thing must behave according to its nature. Fish swim, birds fly.

Every creature except man follows an instinctive pattern of behavior. They have a built-in rule book. They are born to their "station in life," and there is little they can do to change it.

But every man is different. In fact every man is different from every other man. He has a free will and there are almost no limitations on how far above the crowd he can raise his personal stature.

To reach or even approach his potential, man must have something no other creature can even imagine—he must have personal freedom. Without it he can live, subservient to the will of others, but the level of material welfare in an economy without personal freedom is always low. Without the incentive of possible improvement he will not make the effort to increase his individual productivity.

Proof that man must be free is found in the fact that no man can be long forced to do anything that he is truly unwilling to do.

Experience with slave labor shows that man will cut off his own hands, smash his legs, or even take his own life.

Freedom of choice and action is a major stimulant for human imagination and energy. Every man has his own preferences and goals, and, to express and realize these, he must be free to be himself.

The key to individual freedom is the type of government under which man lives. The chief concern of good government— one that stimulates the productivity needed for a high standard of living—is to establish and protect the highest degree of personal freedom possible within a framework of law. A government that does not guarantee this freedom severely retards the improvement of the material welfare of its people.

The differing effects of freedom and of regimentation upon economic efficiency may be seen by comparing the systems of the United States and of the Soviet Union.

Americans are free to dream, plan, try, fail, and try again. Most Soviet citizens must do as they are told, take what is given them, or face punishment as "enemies of the state." In contrast to Americans, most Soviet citizens live very poorly.

There is a scientific explanation for the superior economic performance of free man. It is called: "the results of divergent phenomena," meaning that much progress happens accidently when two or more things are combined without any previous knowledge of what will happen.

Under freedom there are thousands of divergent phenomena coming together in a never-ending stream of imaginative experimentation.

Although most of these experiments are "failures," there are always a few that set off a train of events that result in more and better production of the good things of life.

# MAN PROSPERS THROUGH
# VOLUNTARY COOPERATION

Because of the advantages of the natural division of labor, maximum economic production requires effective cooperation between the people contributing their functions to any given process. Man prospers not alone. That is a law of life that is not subject to change, but man is free to try. He has free will, and in a free society, freedom of choice and the power to decide what he considers his rightful duty in a particular joint or team effort. If he fails to pull his weight, he might get thrown off the team, but no one can force him to do what he is unwilling to do.

But there is another kind of pressure that tends to make him cooperate—public opinion. This pressure, present in every civilization, is based in part on the principle that man should do unto others as he would have others do unto him.

This principle, however, is easier to agree with than to follow. No nation, not even the United States of America, has ever come close to its potential prosperity because so much energy has been devoted to tearing down instead of building up. The selfish desire to win special privilege, regardless of its effect on others, has cost the human race immeasurable amounts of un-created wealth. We cannot fully prosper without helping others prosper.

There is hope in the fact that much non-cooperation stems from ignorance of the facts. No one's judgement can be any better than his information.

Ignorance, by definition, means a lack of knowledge of the facts. In addition, misinterpretation occurs when one or both parties do not understand words as they are used by the "other side."

This points up a requisite for settling economic and other disputes—both parties should be sure they are talking about the same things. Otherwise, as in a serious dispute between labor and management, ignorance of the true values involved makes it easy for both sides to lose their tempers, stop talking and start fighting.

Strikes are like wars—they occur when talking has failed and negotiations have broken off. In strikes, as in wars, both sides most often lose more than they could possibly stand to gain. Yet, wars and strikes continue to be principal reasons for economic waste.

There are, of course, men who for selfish reasons have no intention of cooperating. But most men will when they see and weigh the facts. Lack of cooperation, therefore, is caused largely by lack of clear communication. And, to repeat, no one's judgement is better than his information.

A common economic vocabulary, understandable by all, is one of the keys to a level of prosperity of which man has only dreamed.

# THE IMPORTANCE OF RUNNING SCARED

If primitive man had not learned to be afraid—afraid of ferocious animals, fire, flood, heat, cold, disease, and famine—he would not have survived.

Such fear is not cowardice; it is caution, prudence, common sense, and foresight. Any philosophy that involves total freedom from fear—at any stage of man's development—invites individual and collective disaster.

Reasonable fear will always be important to man's progress. The things to be afraid of have changed greatly, but the need for reasonable fear has not.

Every man in a free society should have two basic fears. First is the fear of personal failure, of being unable to make an economic contribution that attracts the monetary rewards needed for his comfort and security and that of his dependents. Second is the fear of a too-powerful government that could restrict or destroy his freedom.

An appreciation for the first fear should start in the pre-school years and then continue in the classroom where youngsters are given the opportunity to learn how to read, to calculate, to communicate, and to develop their reasoning faculties. It is here, very frequently, that the individual develops the habit of success or the habit of failure. Hopefully, he will develop the habit of success and seek the pleasure of achievement for achievement's sake and the deep satisfaction of a job well done.

Schoolroom experiences often set the pattern for adult life. "Born losers" often develop out of continuing failures. They approach the problem of making a living with the same negative attitude, find it hard to hold a job, and frequently come to feel that the fault is not theirs, but society's.

The second fear, that of a too-powerful government, should start in the classroom where instruction should establish the truth of the adage: "Eternal vigilance is the price of freedom." As shall be shown later in detail, even the best government is naturally, inevitably, and inescapably the enemy of the citizen's freedom.

This is really no one's fault because the natural desire to grow and expand is just as strong in the hearts of those in government as it is in the hearts of private citizens. To achieve this ambition, government officials must constantly try to increase their power over the lives of the people by doing more things for them. And most government officials do this with the encouragement and at the request of private citizens.

It is difficult for the average citizen to recognize this danger because the actions seem to be taken for his benefit. Through the growth of government, the citizen thinks he makes the burdens of freedom less burdensome and lightens the load of responsibility and self-determination. The price he pays for this is diminished personal freedom of choice, and he may ultimately become a ward of the state.

. History shows that this process has contributed to the destruction of great civilizations, such as those in ancient Greece and Rome. Man's age-old challenge has been to develop a government strong enough to protect him but not strong enough to enslave him.

# MAN'S NEED FOR PRIVATE PROPERTY

Legal recognition and protection of free man's natural right to acquire, hold, use, or get paid for the use of private property is one of the essentials of any economy that is striving to achieve the best possible life for its people.

As a stimulus for hard, sustained, imaginative, constructive work, it has no equal. Any society that tries to get along without it will never make the best use of its natural resources, manpower, and tools.

The desire for private property, whatever its form, is deeply rooted in the nature of man and his purpose for living. It is an extension of his personal freedom and a necessary instrument of human dignity.

To destroy man's desire for private property is to destroy his self-respect and his hope for self-improvement.

There are two distinct types of private property—that which is used to produce comfort and pleasure for the owner and his family, and that which is used to produce goods and services to be sold to others. Both types are important to man's life, but the second, in the long run, is most important to continuing improvement in the public welfare.

To fully understand the last statement we must consider every kind of productive property as a tool used either in production or exchange.

To paraphrase Shakespeare, private property used for production is thrice blest—it blesseth those who are the owners, those who make their living using it, and those of the general public who, as customers, benefit from the goods and services produced.

And there is another blessing. Payments for the use of existing tools (profits) provide money that is used to create additional tools.

For best economic results in any nation, the opportunity to acquire, hold, and use private property should be open to every man regardless of color, creed, or the station in life to which he is born. The Constitution that made the Thirteen Colonies into the United States of America carefully provided this opportunity for all citizens. It was the first place in the world where the humblest man could aspire to be anything he thought he could be. "From rags to riches" was part of the original American Dream and still is, and although we have not yet fully realized this goal, we are still pursuing it. That ideal can be stated very simply: it does not matter who or what your father was; the question is what you are.

This sounds corny until we stop to think that, even today, there are very few places in the world where this opportunity exists.

# THE NATURAL ACCEPTANCE
# OF HUMAN INEQUALITY
# AND WHAT HAPPENS TO IT

One of the first things a child observes and accepts as being natural is that there are among his fellows those who are smarter or faster or stronger than he is.

As he goes through school, he notes that these inequalities reach into every phase of life and that certain people move into positions of leadership, seemingly without effort. He reads in the Declaration of Independence that "all men are created equal," but that does not change his acceptance of the vast differences in individual mental and physical performance, and in some cases, vast differences in social and economic rewards.

It is not until people are mentally conditioned through experience to resent the success of others that animosity begins to exercise its destructive impact on society.

This normally does not happen in areas of life with which people are completely familiar. No one resents seeing a famous golfer win $50,000 for three days work in a tournament. In fact, millions of golfers who will never break 100 applaud his success.

Let us examine a hypothetical situation in which people could be "taught" to resent their former hero. Assume that he has used much of his winnings to set himself up in various businesses with the hope that they will earn money for him when he can no longer play tournament golf. One of these companies makes golf slacks bearing his name. Let us use this company as an example of how admiration and respect can be turned into resentment.

To start with, wage scales in the garment industry have always been lower than in many others. Rigorous competition and the relative simplicity of operations have kept it that way. Now suppose a politician or union organizer starts telling the firm's employees and the community's population that the millionaire-golfer-turned-manufacturer "sweats his labor" and takes out as much in profit as he hands out in payroll.

These charges concern an area of activity about which most people know little or nothing. The truth is that the payroll in such a plant is usually ten times as big as the profit. But formal accounting language and procedures make it very hard to prove this to the man in the street and the worker in the plant.

If technical accounting language were discarded and the operation reported in simple, functional words that everyone could understand, the truth would be easy to demonstrate. If the true profit figure were to be indisputably established, the owner of the plant would emerge as a new kind of hero: a creator of jobs, a payer of good wages, and an earner of a fair return on the savings he has put into the business.

It is amazing that most businesses that are under the gun as profiteers will not take the trouble to compile a simple report that refutes false information and restores good will and public acceptance of their success. Failure to do this accounts for much of the economic friction in the United States today.

# THE NECESSITY FOR
# "CAUSE AND EFFECT" THINKING

Most of the progress of primitive man was made possible by his capacity for "cause and effect" thinking. When he touched a hot stone and burned his hand, he learned that heat causes burns. That was simple enough. But as man progressed and his life became more complicated, cause and effect thinking became more difficult.

The things he could not understand from experience, he was forced to rationalize as best he could. For example, disasters were blamed on having offended unfriendly or angry gods. Prayer or sacrifices were considered the only protection against their displeasure. It could be said that man had to stumble upon the causes of good and bad effects and laboriously put them in place. Frequently, the evidence was violently rejected. Scientific discoveries that contradicted accepted "facts" were officially denied, and some of the scientists were considered dangerous lunatics. Some were forbidden to publish or preach their theories, others were even put in jail. The acceptance of new knowledge never comes easily.

Closely related to cause and effect thinking is what is known as a categorical syllogism. This is simply the name given to a proposition with two premises that contain a common term and that lead to a conclusion. If the form of the syllogism is correct and these two premises are true, then the conclusion is valid. While this seems simple, one must be sure that the premises are correct and the form of the syllogism is valid. For example, it is correct to say: all dogs have four legs; Pluto is a dog; therefore Pluto has four legs. But it is incorrect to say: Fido is a black dog; Pluto is a dog; therefore Pluto is black. Note that we have introduced an extra term–black–making the form of the syllogism invalid.

Nevertheless, this type of mistake is regularly made in our day-to-day life. Here is an illustration: Lazy Tom Jones is poor; John Smith is poor; therefore John Smith is lazy.

In this case, it is the thinker who is lazy and who not only does not seek all the evidence, but is careless in presenting the argument. This easy habit of leap-frogging to incorrect conclusions before getting all the facts causes us to "know" and to act upon many things that are simply not true.

Cause and effect thinking consists of finding out what happened before and what happened after, and determining if there is a causative link. To be accepted as truth, the same result would have to occur every time a particular thing was done.

In modern economic management, this thought process is called double-entry thinking, which necessitates keeping track of where things come from and where they went to. Without this system of record keeping, the orderly management of business and government would be impossible.

But the "where from, where to" principle also applies to other important areas of thinking.

An example from nature: the water that falls to the earth from the sky was previously evaporated by the sun from the earth.

An example from economics: the money that comes to the people from government was previously taken from the people by government.

The inability of people to do this type of thinking is still one of the biggest weaknesses of self-government.

# THE IMPORTANCE OF THE "WORK ETHIC"

The settlers who came from Europe to the wilderness that is now the United States of America were drawn from every walk of life and in the aggregate were not much different from the people in the countries they left. The outstanding economic progress they made can be explained by a quality they brought with them and the extraordinary opportunity to use it in an atmosphere of freedom.

This quality of character has been given a name. It is called "the work ethic," which is basically a moral characteristic. It sounds very simple, being based on an accepted sense of what is right and wrong in economic behavior. Because of the religious upbringing of America's early settlers, the requirements of the work ethic became associated with sin and virtue:

- It is sinful to be lazy and indolent.
- It is sinful to be dishonest in money matters.
- It is sinful not to be self-supporting or to fail to support one's family.
- It is sinful not to be thrifty, and if one has the ability, not to acquire private property, which not only produces income for oneself, but may also provide employment for others.
- It is sinful not to pay an honest day's wage.
- It is sinful not to give one's employer an honest day's work.

This devotion to thrift and honesty paid off in a big way. One of the first things the colonists did after winning their freedom from Great Britain was to honor the war debts they owed to the European nations that had helped them in their struggle.

This surprised the entire civilized world and established the new nation as a safe place to loan capital. This also coincided with the beginning of the Industrial Revolution.

By this time, James Watt had perfected the steam engine, quickly followed by "wonderful" tools powered by this new device for harnessing and utilizing energy. Crude as it would be considered today, the engineering was amazing. Watt's partner, an English manufacturer named Matthew Boulton, took pride in being able to bore a 50-inch cylinder so accurately that it did not "err the thickness of an old shilling in any part."

Power tools provided a substitute for the one thing the infant nation lacked–a sufficient labor force. Mechanical horsepower performed the work of dozens of men, and gave every worker a group of "helpers," each one of which "worked" for about 1/200th of the human wage.

Under these conditions, the work ethic encouraged economic miracles. In about 100 years, hard work, thrift, and the application of profits to new investment advanced the United States from a relatively backward nation to the industrial leader of the world.

It has been said that America's phenomenal growth occurred mainly because of natural resources and waterways. But this is not exactly true. Many other nations had these same advantages and the same opportunities.

The people who came to the New World came to build, and with the help of the work ethic, build they did.

There has been great concern in recent years that the work ethic may be dying. There are, however, signs that the work ethic is not dying but rather requires a little intelligent nurturing. A number of American businesses have experimented with various imaginative approaches designed to give employees more direct incentive and greater participation in decisions that affect their work. When carefully planned, programs have been highly successful: one mirror manufacturer was able to cover successive annual wage and benefit increases of 11%, 9%, and 5.5% through increased productivity and cost reduction, and these were also substantial enough to permit making price reductions to customers and to absorb rising costs of materials.

Stimulation of the desire to produce can still work "miracles."

# WHY IS THE GOLDEN RULE SO WIDELY
# ACCEPTED AND SO RARELY HONORED?

The Achilles Heel of human progress is the larceny that lurks in almost every heart.

Every society publicly supports, in one form or another, the ethic of doing unto others as one would be done to; nevertheless, in matters of money and goods, the temptation to steal or to accept stolen goods seems irresistible.

Even thieves know that stealing is damaging to society. It may not appear so at first glance, but the knowing acceptance of stolen goods is equally damaging. The latter may or may not involve actual goods. But it almost always involves money, and it can take a number of forms.

Of these, extortion and bribery are the simplest to understand. Conviction of public officials and employees throughout the nation for these offenses illustrate that the receipt of illegal income by many groups of public servants has too often become a way of life for many. The "gravy", "graft", or the "skim" is considered a traditional part of their income. Lately, however, the American people, increasingly convinced that something can be done about it, have become much less tolerant of this kind of behavior. This attitude has led to numerous convictions of public officials "on the take."

But there is a more pervasive and potentially dangerous form of larceny that is entirely legal but ethically questionable. To illustrate it, let us assume a simple hypothetical situation. A village must have a new well and water pump on the public square. A town meeting is called for public discussion and decision. The drilling and the pump would cost $1,000. There are, in this town, 100 citizens, all of whom own property and are either present or represented. Let us further assume that all will have roughly equal need for water.

A brisk debate develops around the question of which citizens should be assessed for how much of the $1,000.

One point of view is that since everyone has equal need for

and access to the water, every citizen should be assessed $10.

Another view is that assessments should be made according to how much property each citizen owns. In other words, those with more property would pay more for their water.

A third view is that the people owning the largest amounts of property should pay the entire amount; while no one would probably say it this baldly, the rationale is that it is easier for them to pay.

The decision will be made by popular vote.

This situation presents in ultra-simple form one of the more perplexing problems of self-governing nations. The majority have the legal right, by their votes, to spend money belonging to the minority for the majority's benefit.

Suppose they put the burden on the large property holders. Would you call this stealing? Certainly not in a criminal context. Would you call it larceny? This is harder to deny. After all, members of the majority have voted themselves benefits for which they will not pay. Would you call it receiving stolen goods? Not in the technical sense because the goods are taken away with public approval. Nevertheless, behind that public approval is the aforementioned larceny.

Regardless of what you call it, when this legal larceny reaches certain proportions, the effect on the national economy can be devastating. Since they can clearly see that they are being penalized for their success, the gifted people capable of creating essential wealth are likely to simply stop creating.

# DOES MATERIALISM
# DESTROY IDEALISM?

For decades it has been popular for economic reformers interested in establishing greater "social justice" and stepping up the war on poverty to downgrade the process by which one accumulates wealth and the actual accumulation. The emphasis varies from critic to critic, but essentially, these criticisms revolve around the contention that the process blunts sensitivity, destroys idealism, and lessens proper concern for the underprivileged.

The "money-grubbing" United States is the main target of criticism because of its "devotion to profit."

The argument bears closer examination.

Since the dawn of history, most men have tried to improve their conditions by acquiring physical things whether they be caves or ranch houses, camels or automobiles, wheelbarrows or motor trucks (the less a man has, the more materialistic he has to be).

Many of our early ancestors–the poor immigrants who came from Europe to transform a wilderness into a good place to live– had to be very materialistic to avoid starving or freezing to death. And, in the beginning, many of them starved or froze.

Later, when there was some surplus that might have been given away, they used it to acquire better tools that enabled them to produce more in less time with less physical labor. This meant that they had to produce more than they consumed and to deny themselves some immediate comfort and pleasure. This, too, was materialistic. It could quite accurately be characterized as "devotion to profit."

As a matter of hard fact, it is this "devotion to profit" that made it possible for the United States to become the most generous, idealistic nation in the world today.

The word "profit" comes from the word "progress," meaning an increase in physical wealth. The word "wealth" comes from the word "welfare."

American wealth is private wealth, privately produced, and,

until recently, largely privately used. Today, the progressive income tax provides the Federal government with billions of dollars to prove how idealistic it is possible to be as a result of "devotion to profit" by "money-grubbing" citizens.

Taxes come out of private wealth. Concern for the underprivileged usually takes the form of the redistribution of tax dollars. So it is the "anti-idealistic" profit motive that produces the wherewithal to finance idealism.

But there is more to it than this. The American people are not only the richest in the world; they are also the most generous. The billions of dollars contributed to the arts, religion, education, medical research—just to mention a few—are private profit dollars and certainly must be considered idealistic dollars.

The most certain way to create more underprivileged people is to destroy the privilege of creating and using private wealth.

# MAN'S NEED FOR
# REASONABLE INSECURITY

Man is a thinking, incurably curious, competitive, habitually risk-taking creature. He wants reasonable security and stability, but is incapable of being contented in completely static circumstances.

The most obvious example of complete economic security is life in prison. The price is freedom, and that price is intolerable. Perhaps less obvious, but basically similar, is life in a totalitarian state where the promise of economic security is extended by the state at a price of absolute obedience. Some citizens seem to like this, but the disciplinary and penal problems of dictatorial nations indicate that the vast majority of citizens would prefer to make most of their own decisions, economic and otherwise, and have the satisfaction of trying to make them work. The feeling of reasonable insecurity stems from man's knowledge that, without his best efforts, he will probably fall short of his goal. This is an essential challenge.

Much has been said about the hostile attitude of American youth toward the competitive economy into which they were born. Many feel this attitude is instilled in the classroom where very few kind words or thoughts are expressed concerning the system of competitive free enterprise. This system is often unjustly characterized as being "money grubbing," "dog-eat-dog," and unresponsive to human needs.

But scores of credible surveys indicate that the work-and-win tradition still motivates most of our young people. This can be observed when specific economic reforms are being proposed. In 1969, the subject of the annual college poll was guaranteed income. On April 6th of that year, the New York Daily News reported the following reactions from universities located in eleven different parts of the nation:

- Harvard–"It's an invitation not to work."

- Case Western Reserve–"Another case of something for nothing."

- Rochester–"Most people don't need it. Those who do, would abuse it."
- City College of New York–"It's a joke."
- Occidental–"Makes a man think he's doing a job, but it's just a hand-out."
- San Francisco–"No one can believe in himself if he is supported by relief or by wages he does not earn."
- Miami of Ohio–"Next we will be guaranteed a new car."
- Stanford–"Let them earn their wages like every other American."

From Notre Dame came what seemed to be the consensus– "We'll only become the great nation we should be when all people have an opportunity to work and earn their own way in life."

The mind and energies of man are most stimulated when facing a challenge of his own choice with a reasonable chance of success. The chance of failure must be ever-present to insure his best efforts.

Individual happiness lies not in security; it lies in progress toward goals of one's own choosing. When one "has it made," one makes nothing.

The secret of free man's continued progress is that he is never satisfied with past achievements. Nothing is so good that it might not be improved. And the chance–even a risky chance– of making progress, is the never-ending challenge of life.

# SUBSIDIZED IDLENESS –
# THE DRUG THAT NOBODY KNOWS

Every civilization on record has made use of alcohol or other drugs. When these drugs are used to excess, they can bring on changes in character, personality, and behavior.

But modern industrialized man faces the problem of a new drug that is not medicinal, but is much more destructive of character. It is subsidized idleness over long periods of time–public support of the chronically unemployed.

In 1960, Dr. M. Harvey Brenner, a sociologist at Yale University, completed a monumental 50-year statistical study of mental health in the United States. He concluded that: "doctors can forecast the general state of mental health with a glance at society's unemployment figure."

This presents a truly difficult problem because in a balanced economy, to avoid chronic wage inflation, there must be a few more people looking for jobs than there are jobs looking for people. Fortunately, most unemployment is too brief to have a psychological impact, but long term unemployment is devastating. To the normal man who wakes up in the morning with nothing useful to do, and nowhere to go where he is needed, life becomes a nightmare out of which he must either make some sense or lose his senses.

The sense he often makes out of it is that he is one of those special persons to whom the world owes a living. And if the living is not as good as he thinks he deserves, his resentment against society knows no bounds.

The tragic irony of subsidized idleness is the humanitarian spirit in which it is dispensed. In truth, nothing is more inhumane than destroying the fabric of a man's character. This way of life burns away two cardinal virtues and needs of man–his self-respect and his self-reliance. Psychologically, it has the subconscious guilt-producing impact of receiving stolen goods.

After a certain length of time, according to mental health experts, living on relief puts a man or woman virtually beyond hope of rehabilitation.

The industrialized nations have been so busy creating wealth

–and have found it so easy to get the money needed to subsidize idleness–that the problem has been swept under the rug. But no economy, however strong, no system, however dynamic, can long avoid its deadening influence on the national character.

This essay presents the problem but not the solution. But one thing is certain: unless useful, satisfying work can be found for every able-bodied person, prosperity will continue to nourish the seeds of its own destruction.

# SELF-DISCIPLINE –
## KEY TO PROGRESS UNDER FREEDOM

Man's progress involves a simple train of thought:

- His material welfare is based on civilization.

- Civilization is based on law and order.

- Law and order are based on discipline.

- There are two basic types of discipline–that which is imposed by others and that which is self-imposed.

- Discipline must be imposed upon children to form the personal habits that make for self-discipline; it must also be imposed upon adults who do not impose it upon themselves.

Now consider the fact that, in the United States, discipline has increasingly come to be considered obsolete and unenforceable. This revolution started in the classroom under the label of "progressive education," which encourages children to do what "comes naturally." This educational philosophy spread to the home as parents were advised that forcing children to do things they did not want to do created anti-social attitudes and stunted development of the "whole child." This philosophy frowns upon making embarrassing comparisons of the scholastic achievement of one child with another, and holds that most anti-social behavior results from forces for which the individual is not personally responsible.

The result of this "permissive philosophy" has been to discourage teachers, confuse parents and their children, and alarm police authorities. Mass education has never been more chaotic. Adult respect for the principles and institutions underlying American civilization has never been so low nor have crime rates ever been so high.

One good thing, however, has happened. The excesses of the lawless minority have finally shocked the nation into realizing what is happening and seem to be crystallizing the greatest of all social forces–public indignation in a free society. From all indications, the importance of discipline and law enforcement are being rediscovered.

This does not mean that the American people either do or should believe that all the existing laws are perfect, but they should have a basic respect for law. If individuals feel that any given law is in need of improvement, they have the right and the duty to try to have it changed; as long as it is on the books, however, it should be obeyed. Any society in which anyone can decide with impunity which laws are to be obeyed is headed for history's scrap pile.

This fact is well-known to professional radicals. This small minority hopes to use violence to reduce American civilization to chaos before our "decadent society" rises up in self-defense. The majority has taken legal countersteps to combat violence.

Unfortunately, some of the steps being demanded by members of the outraged majority may go too far and damage or destroy the right to dissent that is necessary for the progress and very existence of any democratic society.

But there must be enough discipline to make orderly life possible, and people who do not discipline themselves within the framework of the law must be disciplined by others. This must be done with fairness and restraint. We must not destroy freedom in our efforts to preserve the discipline necessary for a successful society.

# WHY GREAT CIVILIZATIONS COLLAPSE

Regarding the "state" of any nation there is a difference between the emotional approach of "viewing with alarm" and viewing as a result of realistic cold-blood appraisal. From the first viewpoint any change seems threatening, whether the change is for the better or the worse. From the second viewpoint, it is pinpointing specific changes and logically examining their impact. Viewing it realistically, just how strong is the United States of America, how well is it prepared to hold its own in an envious, troubled, and hostile world?

The economic indicators look good. We have enormous productive capacity. American-made goods are still good bargains despite the inflationary wage-price spiral.

The human considerations are not so favorable. There are definite signs of deterioration in individual character, the sum total of which is the national character.

Patriotism, one of the load-bearing pillars of any strong nation, is on the wane. Many Americans have turned their backs on the sentiment expressed by Oliver Wendell Holmes: "One flag, one land, one heart, one hand, one nation ever more!"

The credibility gap between people and government has created a feeling of cynicism.

Industriousness, the willingness to accept personal responsibility and do constructive work that adds to the wealth of the economy, is becoming the desire to do as little work as possible for as much money as possible. Voluntary unemployment has become common. Improved tools, so far, have helped to bridge the productivity gap, but cannot do so forever.

Observance of the law has reached an all-time low. Since 1960, the reported incidence of violent crime has increased 57%, robbery 70%, property crime 73%. Were the reporting more accurate, these figures would undoubtedly be much higher.

The use of escape drugs is too prevalent to be measured.

Family solidarity is falling apart. Chastity is "old hat." Having illegitimate children—"father unknown"—is becoming for some a profitable way of life.

Youthful respect and admiration for the American way of life and its basic institutions, now disparagingly called "The Establishment" or "The System," are turning into doubt and disapproval.

All of these patterns of behavior can be classified as personal or public immorality, and they bring to mind a statement by the famous historian, Arnold Toynbee, who wrote: "Of the 22 (defunct) civilizations that appear in history, 19 of them collapsed when they reached the moral state the United States is in now."

Just as sick people often reject the possibility of death, "sick" nations tend to deny their "sickness."

We are not predicting the death of the American Dream, but we submit that unless the American people, as individuals, determine to become better people, it can and will "happen here."

The schools cannot reverse this trend; the churches cannot do it; the government cannot do it. Only the people themselves, through self-examination, self-education, and self-improvement can do it.

What will the historians write about America one hundred years from now?

# FREEDOM'S GREATEST SAFEGUARD –
## CRITICISM AND DISSENT

The men who drafted the Constitution of the United States were among the wisest, most capable, and best prepared scholars that ever came together on a joint project. They knew history and human nature and what used to be called political economics— the art of government.

It is no accident that the First Amendment guaranteed to the people the right of free speech, the right to criticize, and the right to dissent. They knew that these are not only the greatest safe-guards to freedom and progress, but that without them you do not have freedom.

Any government, society, or institution not subject to constant evaluation and criticism will not be made aware of the things it needs to know to make good decisions, and will be weakened and perhaps destroyed by its own self-satisfaction. This could happen even to our wonderfully productive private property system.

Some people believe that criticism of the American way of life has gone too far and that the spirit of dissent has become destructive. Some critics, of course, are deliberately destructive. For reasons best known to themselves, they want to "improve" things by destroying them. But they are the exception, not the rule.

It is true that the so-called "Establishment" is under strong attack by the younger generation, but the spirit of dissent is a sincere desire to improve, not to destroy.

But if the "Establishment" does not meet the challenge, improve communication with the dissidents, and emerge stronger and better because of it, some of the criticism must be well-grounded.

As of 1973, only 44% of the public expressed "confidence" in higher education, 36% in organized religion, and 29% in "big business."

Assuming that this lack of confidence is not justified, the burden of proof lies on the criticized and not on the critics. Part of the reason for disapproval must be poor communication, and it must be remembered that no one's judgement can be any better than his information.

Members of the "Establishment" also have freedom of speech. In the case of big business, there is no doubt that communication has been poor. While the truth has been consistently published for the sophisticated reader, for the general public, the technical words and phrases used might as well be a foreign language.

Continued freedom of enterprise in our free nation depends upon continued public approval–"the wisdom of the people." Big business, as a justifiable factor in the economy, may not feel any obligation to meet dissent with dissent, but management's silence could well be interpreted as consent.

Freedom of speech is a two-way street, and in a successful democracy, must be used as such.

# THE EVOLUTION
# OF PRODUCTION

# MAKING AND USING STONE AGE TOOLS
## Living Site (Les Eyzies, France) Drawing Based on Archeological Evidence

ROCK PAINTINGS
made about 20,000 years ago
as preserved in the caves
of Lascaux, France

DEATH AT A DISTANCE.
Improved throwing spears
and bows and arrow made
hunting more productive.

SAWING

DRILLING HOLES OR FIRE MAKING
by use of a bow string to spin the drill.

GRINDING
wild grain and seeds
with mortar and pestle.

CHIPPING AND
BURNISHING
to form stone
bowls.

WITH THIS
"FIST AXE"
the hunter could
make spears, skin
animals, cut up meat
and do many other
jobs of work.

SCRAPING A PELT
to prepare animal hide.

THE END PRODUCT OF THE HUNTERS
WAS MEAT FOR FOOD, FAT FOR LIGHTING,
AND HIDES FOR CLOTHING AND SHELTER.

PRESSURE FLAKING
to make sharp-edged flint tools.

# PRODUCTIVITY IN THE STONE AGE

Through our eyes today, the family group illustrated on the facing page seems to have an incredibly low standard of living. The picture warrants careful study. It represents a composite of the typical life style of our ancestors over a very long period during the latter part of the Stone Age. The form of civilization was established by Stone Age man in performing work operations shown here. The tools used for these operations are extensions of the hand, and modern machine tools are extensions of these stone tools.*

Going back in man's history for more than 40,000 years, scientists find that the size of the average person's brain was comparable to the average size of that of people today. Yet, progress over thousands of years was extremely slow.

The reason for this very slow improvement lies in the fact that man's material welfare depends upon his productivity, which hinges upon the quality of his tools, which in turn depends upon how hard he thinks about them.

The ability to "imagine" better tools has always been the key to man's material progress. It is called "conceptual thinking."

Anthropologists do not agree on the reasons for the steady and concurrent improvement of man's mind and of his tools. But, it is accepted as fact that the making and using of stone tools was the catalyst responsible for bringing about civilization.

Did the mental progress come naturally and bring about conceptual tool thinking, or did the nagging inconvenience of poor tools force the brain to keep on thinking and through this exercise, repeated in one generation after another for thousands of generations, weed out all but those individuals who became better able to think? Here is a simple example of why the latter theory is regarded as the most significant.

The use of most stone tools held in the hand caused constant fatigue and occasional pain. The hunter in the picture is holding a "fist-axe," and its rough, jagged shape illustrates one of the problems encountered with this type of hand-held tool. In using this tool, this physical limitation could not be ignored by the mind.

Every time a man using a fist-axe banged his fingers, his brain automatically asked: "Isn't there a better way?" It took billions of bangs, but finally someone's mind conceived the idea of putting a handle on the fist-axe. It undoubtedly took many generations lost in the mist of prehistoric time to develop ways to securely fasten the axe-head to a handle so it would not fall off every time he tried to use it. The handle gave leverage, and was not only more comfortable to use, but enabled the user to multiply the force he would apply with the cutting edge, resulting in greater production.

Another example illustrates how conceptual thinking generates a new tool and then the improved tool expands man's opportunities. Man has always tried to avoid the necessity of thinking. The invention of the bow and arrow did not occur until about 25,000 years ago. The constant dangers and the extra effort and limitations of "close-up" killing forced him to dwell upon this problem, searching his brain for a better way to hunt.

The bow multiplied the power of the hunter's muscle. It built up energy and stored that energy for a short period, until released as a powerful thrust upon the arrow. This was a tremendous breakthrough because it introduced "long distance" killing.

The bow and arrow was much safer than throwing a spear and greatly increased the scope and productivity of man's hunting activities. The bow and arrow also made it possible for man to hunt by himself instead of as a dependent in close cooperation with other members of an organized group.

One effect of the bow and arrow was that people could migrate with a greater assurance of a food supply. Barter between tribes increased. People from one tribe mingled with people from other tribes, and inter-marriage broadened the gene pool. As population grew, the stream of life expanded as it flowed on, gathering momentum through mutations introduced from many different tribes.

When our early ancestors learned how to manufacture ("manus," hand, plus "facere," make) cutting edges in stone either by using the percussion method or the pressure method of flaking, and later to finely hone them with suitable abrasive materials, his tool progress was rapid. This was particularly true of tools for his most important economic activity, hunting. Weapons were highly refined and varied. Every type of animal was successfully hunted ranging from the fleet-footed to huge mastodons, and great progress was also made in developing fishing skills.

The word Neolithic ("Neo" new, plus "Lithic" stone) describes the last phase of the Stone Age. Neolithic tools were polished smooth and had cutting edges straight from end to end, which could be kept sharp by additional honing and polishing. They did better work than the tools made by pressure flaking, which left sharp but jagged edges that could not be resharpened, and such tools when dull, had to be thrown away and new ones made.

Neolithic tools made it possible to do more refined types of production such as crude carpentry, weaving, and pottery.

These advances in living standards were accompanied by the development of systematic agriculture starting about 9,000 years ago. With the improved stone tools to work with, man was able to grow a variety of foods, starting with wheat, barley, and millet, which better enabled him to assure himself of a reasonably steady supply of these types of food.

In Egypt and surrounding Near East areas, simple hoe cultivation was combined with an animal-using economy. In some areas, there are indications that animal husbandry preceeded agriculture.

While Stone Age man had used dogs for hunting, the domestication of work-animals brought the first "living tools" to help the human muscle work. Primitive agriculture made possible the village, which was to be the base for future civilization.

When we say that the Stone Age man had, at a primitive level, all of the basic economic problems we have today, it might be thought that we have left out a key factor–money. As a matter of fact, money has nothing to do with production. Money is nothing but numbers stamped or printed on metal or paper and used to count physical things and measure their production cost compared with that of other things. The true measurement of cost was the number of work hours required for gathering food and material for production. Early man, through experience, came to know this and was constantly applying this principle as he made choices as to where and how he would apply his work time. His economic priorities had to be very much like ours. Food had to come first. Shelter and clothing were next. That took care of the basic things needed for survival.

And upon being relatively assured of survival, his thoughts turned to other things. Being inventive by nature, man has always asked himself: "How can I get the things I need without working so hard?" The answer is better tools.

# PRODUCTIVITY IN THE BRONZE AGE

Stone Age man had no knowledge of metals, except for the occasional and very rare find of a meteorite or of a nodule of native pure copper lying on the ground. By 5,000 B.C., copper was known and used for tools, weapons, jewelry, and similar items in Egypt and other Near East areas. Egypt proper had no copper ores, but records show that the rich copper mines in the Sinai Peninsula east of modern-day Cairo were worked by expeditions dispatched by Pharoah Snefru as early as 3,800 B.C. These copper ore deposits played an important role in Egypt's emergence as a great power between the fourth and third millennia, B.C. Copper could be worked and reworked into any shape, would hold a fair edge after "work hardening," and in the form of chisels, axes, and similar tools used in conjunction with diorite pounders and wooden wedges, made possible at great effort, the building of canals, the first Pyramids, temples and palaces, and similar "monumental" projects. But even "work hardened" copper is relatively soft, and not until copper and tin—a metal not at all suitable for weapons or tools—were melted together to form bronze was this drawback overcome.

Earliest known bronze artifacts, thought to be of Sumerian origin, date back to the fourth millennium B.C., and this new metal was probably first obtained by accident. Some ores used by the Sumerians (Mesopotamia) were "stanniferous" (contained both copper and tin), and so melting them to obtain copper would create bronze instead. Nevertheless, tin and copper rarely occur together, and it must have taken tremendous mental effort and much trial-and-error to first identify the vital ingredients, learn to mix them in the proper ratios, ferret out their ore locations, and then arrange to bring them together. Since ancient bronze tools consistently contain the 5 to 15% tin-content necessary to achieve desired characteristics for different uses, man obviously succeeded at a relatively early date in "inventing" Bronze Metallurgy—a truly towering achievement.

While blest with the rich Sinai copper mines, Egypt had no

tin ores. Consequently, although the beginning of the Bronze Age is conventionally dated at about 3,000 B.C., bronze tools did not come into common use in Egypt until about 2,000 B.C. In fact, not until after the Egyptians suffered military defeats at the hands of the Hyksos, who used bronze scimitars and armor, powerful bows, and horse-drawn wheeled chariots, did the Egyptians shift to the general use of bronze tools and weapons. The source of the tin Egypt used to make bronze is not recorded, but she traded throughout the then known world. Once Egypt adopted bronze tools and weapons and the other "foreign" tools of production and warfare, she drove out the Hyksos and again established herself as the dominant power in the Near East, going on to enjoy her greatest period in history, which culminated with the illustrious 67-year reign of Ramses II at the beginning of the thirteenth century B.C.

While bronze was adopted slowly and at varying rates throughout the then known world, tools made of this "magic metal" were so far superior to those made of stone or copper that bronze revolutionized man's methods of production, and ultimately his lifestyle. Things could now be made routinely that previously could only be produced at excessive cost, if at all. Bronze saws and adzes permitted the advanced carpentry necessary to construct the great wooden ships that plied the Nile, carrying huge stones and obelisks as well as commercial cargo, and ventured forth into the Mediterranean Sea. Within a relatively short time, Egypt enjoyed a fantastic upsurge in the manufacture of new things. In addition to the shipbuilding made possible by the superior wood-working qualities of bronze tools over those of stone or copper—which encouraged foreign commerce and increased the exchange of knowledge—bronze also made possible such things as ox-drawn carts and plows and horse-drawn vehicles as well as magnificent statuary and the later huge temples of more advanced refinement and design.

Like virtually everything else, bronze tools were completely under the control of the Pharoah (king), and thus he controlled production. Egypt had great quantities of excellent flint, and peasants tilling the fields still used tools made of flint as late as 1,000 B.C.—but those industries deemed vital by the Pharoah used bronze tools. Through a system of corvee (drafting of citizens to work on public projects) the state bureaucracy managed the workers as if they were slaves, although their religious beliefs told them they were working for their God, who was personified in the Pharoah, and so the records of that time still in existence indicate that they worked well.

No one factor, of course, can account for the success or failure of a complicated civilization such as the one ancient Egypt evolved. Nevertheless, it surely is more than mere coincidence that her two greatest general periods of growth, power, and affluence coincided with her leadership, first in copper tools, then later in bronze tools, and that she went into decline with the advent of the Iron Age. Egypt has no iron ore, and did not succeed in importing sufficient quantities of that new and superior metal to maintain her lofty position of power and greatness.

# PRODUCTIVITY IN THE IRON AGE

The first successful and continuous smelting of iron for making cutting tools and weapons was done by the Hittites about 1500 B.C. in what is now Turkey. The Hittites built a powerful empire utilizing the productivity of the new miracle metal.

As a metal from which to make tools, iron was far superior to bronze and much more plentiful. A craftsman could own the tools he worked with.

The first tools made from iron were not radically different in design from the old bronze tools, but their cutting performance was spectacular, particularly when the ore from which the iron was smelted had an "impurity" content. So was born the idea of changing iron into alloys with superior qualities that later came to be known as steel.

The malleable quality of iron made it ideal for many other things beyond its importance as superior cutting tools. It was forged into horseshoes and made into axles and tires for wagons. It was made into gate hinges, and nails for construction. Thus, the fantastic material and cultural surge of progress during the Greco-Roman era was based not only on the greater production capability of iron hand tools but equally so upon the new uses for iron as the construction material for making products.

The range and scope of uses for iron continued to expand throughout the Middle Age period of European history. Craftsmanship became highly skilled with the emergence of craft guilds. Members of guilds started as apprentices, usually between the ages of ten and fifteen, then moved up to journeyman after one or two years. Apprentices and journeymen worked under a master who taught them the skills of the craft. On the average it took an apprentice seven years to become a master, although many apprentices and journeymen never became masters. Generally, to become a master, a member of a craft guild was required to go through training under a master and to prove his capabilities by examination or the making of a "masterpiece." As a master, a member of a guild earned full membership in his exclusive tradesman club and was able to train apprentices and journeymen.

With the coming of the Industrial Revolution, iron was destined to become the basic structural material of modern civilization.

Melted iron could be poured into sand molds to form the castings used for making steam engines, machine tools, and parts for manufacturing machinery.

Iron billets were forged and rolled into rails for railways and into beams for bridges and for constructing buildings.

Bar stock, strips, and sheets of steel were rolled to specifications desired as the principal building material for the vast array of metal products. The age we live in owes its very existence to one natural resource above any other—iron.

# PROGRESS WAS RAPID
# ONCE MUSCLE POWER COULD BE MULTIPLIED

During the centuries so far discussed, Man's Material Welfare improved at a snail's pace. There was a chronic shortage of food, clothing, and shelter despite the "natural" population controls of famine, disease, and war. With the help of metal tools, man's progress during the past 5,000 years was far more rapid than during the Stone Age. Nevertheless, until man was able to mechanically multiply his muscle power beginning in the late 1700's, his productivity was restricted to what he could produce with that muscle power, work animals, and a limited use of wind and water power.

Because substitutes for muscle power were very limited until about 200 years ago, improvements in the quantity and quality of man's food, clothing, and shelter came slowly prior to that time. While a tiny number of privileged individuals with access to the muscle power of forced labor were able to acquire substantial amounts of both necessities and luxuries, most humans did well if they managed to acquire the bare essentials for survival — and millions failed to do so.

The first Stone Age man who put a handle on a fist-axe was able to add leverage to his muscle power. Modern man, by substituting mechanical power for muscle power, is able to multiply that leverage a thousand fold. The first modern muscle-power substitutes were steam-driven, and they represented a tremendous leap forward. But this development, based on the principle that water, converted into steam and trapped, could become an immensely powerful, controllable substitute for muscle power, had to await the invention of the necessary technology.

The principle was known for thousands of years: it was secretly used by the Greek rulers and high priests of ancient Alexandria to make religious statues belch steam to mystify and frighten their superstitious followers.

But whatever the reason — perhaps because the ancient Greeks and their later intellectual heirs gave a great deal of thought to understanding nature but little to practical use of that understanding, perhaps because slave labor was a satisfactory source of work energy — technology was slow in developing.

A true "steam engine" had to wait for the creation of a steam boiler that would hold pressure and of metal castings accurately finished into sliding parts.

# MAN'S MATERIAL WELFARE
# DEPENDS UPON PRODUCTION

With rare exception—for example, the things nature provides without man's assistance—man's economic welfare depends upon producing the things he needs and wants.

Production has been reduced to a very simple formula: MMW = NR + HE × T. When written out it reads: Man's Material Welfare equals Natural Resources plus Human Energy multiplied by Tools.

Everything man produces is covered by this formula. For a very simplified example, imagine a granite structure in place of MMW, a stone quarry in place of NR, skilled craftsmen in place of HE, and stone-working equipment in place of T.

Obviously, the quantity and quality of man's production depends upon the quantity and quality of his natural resources, his mental and muscular energy, and the tools that multiply that energy.

To better understand the problem of making progress toward improving man's material welfare, let us see how much man can control these factors.

To start with, there is very little man can do about natural resources. Nature and time are responsible for their creation. Man can only find them, extract them, cultivate them, and change their form, condition, and place.

Secondly, the potential for increasing man's human energy is very limited. When highly motivated or stimulated, man is more productive, but if economic progress depended upon human energy alone, very little would take place.

This leads to only one conclusion: the third factor—tools—is the only one that man can increase and improve virtually without limits.

Compare, if you will, a wagon train with a railroad train, a hand shovel with a power shovel, a needle and thread with a sewing machine.

In tool improvement we see the importance of mental energy. New tools start as ideas in the minds of inventors. They begin to take shape through the skills of design engineers. They become fully operative when turned over to production engineers.

But here we can see the importance of the investor, the man who must practice temporary self-denial and divert part of his income from comfort and pleasure and devote it to financing the inventors and the engineers.

In a free society, people become investors because, if the project is successful, they can expect to be paid for the use of their

# THE COMMON DENOMINATORS

## NATURAL RESOURCES + HUMAN ENERGY

NR PLUS HE MULTIPLIED

For the sake of simplicity, the end product in this illustrated formula is a flag-pole base made entirely of *one* material—granite. Also, the form and condition are changed with simple one-purpose tools. Regardless of what the end product might be, this formula and principle of the law of production applies money. These payments are variously called profits, dividends, and interest, and are the foundation of what is called the profit system. It should be called the profit and loss system because in any new development the risk of loss is ever-present.

In the industrial sector of modern economies, tools provide most of the work-energy consumed. In the United States today, tools do more than 95% of the work performed. That is why it leads the world in productivity.

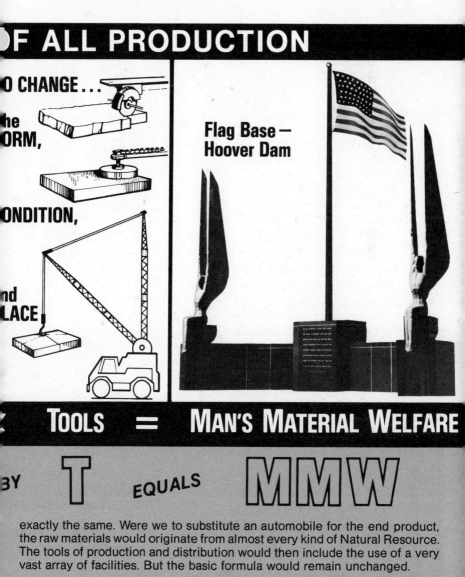

## OF ALL PRODUCTION

O CHANGE...

he
ORM,

ONDITION,

nd
LACE

Flag Base —
Hoover Dam

## TOOLS = MAN'S MATERIAL WELFARE

BY  T  EQUALS  MMW

exactly the same. Were we to substitute an automobile for the end product, the raw materials would originate from almost every kind of Natural Resource. The tools of production and distribution would then include the use of a very vast array of facilities. But the basic formula would remain unchanged.

# HOW MAN PRODUCES

As we have seen, tools are the only factor in the production formula that man can control. Increases can be limitless both in quantity and quality. But the process is neither easy nor rapid.

Tools come into being in a free society only when men are willing to postpone present comforts for the expectations of future returns. They do this when (1) their property is safe from seizure, and (2) they will, in all likelihood, get paid for its use. The free market (unregulated and with competitive supply and free expression of demand) determines what is produced.

In contrast, tools come into being in a state controlled society at any time the government decides to use tax money or other government funds for this purpose. The decision as to what the tools will be used to produce is made by government planners not on the basis of what the people want, but on the basis of what these planners believe the people should have.

All things used by man to change the form, condition, and place of natural resources are tools.

Arable land is a tool. Hand implements are tools. Factory buildings are tools, as is the land under them. Obviously factory machines are tools. Ships, boats, and aircraft used in production and exchange are tools. And invested money is also a tool because it is required in the process of production and exchange.

The wages of people making their living using tools are the principal cost of production. Tools become obsolete when better tools become available, and in a progressive economy, the older, less productive tools must be discarded and replaced by the newer, more efficient tools. Otherwise the selling price of the product may become too high to be competitive with that of comparable products produced by newer tools.

This sometimes happens on a national scale. Previous to 1900, Great Britain was the world's foremost industrial nation. But she neglected to keep her tools up to date while the United States was using only the most modern tools. As a result, by the turn of the century, England dropped out of first place and the United States became preeminent.

Today, America faces the same situation Great Britain faced three-quarters of a century ago: the updating of tools is being neglected.

# STEAM POWER –
## MAN'S RELEASE FROM HARD LABOR

Thousands of seventeenth century engineers knew that, under the right circumstances, enormous power could be created by turning water into steam and condensing it back to water. The problem was to trap the steam and direct its force against a movable part that would activate other parts.

Hundreds of these men must have thought long and hard about this fundamentally simple but mechanically frustrating problem. Two of these were Englishmen, Thomas Newcomen and Thomas Savery, who in 1705, developed a working steam engine that was an improvement on a rudimentary model with no moving parts, patented by Savery in 1698. The up-and-down motion of the steam-powered machine, named after Newcomen, suited it for pumping operations, and the first recorded install-ment of a "miner's friend" was on a Worstershire colliery in 1712. The design proved highly reliable but extremely inefficient—it utilized less than 1% of its fuel energy—and most of the several hundred machines built over the next 50 years were used to pump out coal mines using low grade, "unsalable" coal, although some were used to pump water supplies for towns or to feed in-dustrial waterwheels.

About fifty years after that first installment, a Scottish in-strument maker named James Watt was called in to repair a Newcomen engine. He saw three ways to improve it: he added the flywheel, the sliding arm and valve, and invented a rotary motion to do the driving. In 1765, Watt developed a new type of condenser, insulated to reduce heat loss, that cut fuel consump-tion by 75%.

Watt's design of the steam engine utilized steam pressure on both ends of a piston, with a valve alternately cycling steam to first one end of the piston and then to the other, creating the reciprocal action necessary to perform continuous useful work.

His innovations made the steam engine practical for applica-tions other than pumping water. Still, the first of the engines were not put to work until 1776, a year after John Wilkinson invented a necessary manufacturing machine tool: the boring mill.

Capital to finance Watt's work was provided by a wealthy man named Matthew Boulton, who became his partner. The partnership of Boulton and Watt was a highly successful enterprise that produced 496 engines between 1776 and 1800, when the basic steam engine patent expired and Watt retired.

Thus, the steam engine passed through the usual cycle of every new mechanical invention: (1) conception, (2) practicality, (3) financing, and (4) tooling up. All four steps were essential to perhaps the most significant labor-saving breakthrough in the economic history of man.

Furthermore, it cannot be said that any one of the four men involved was the least or the most important. Indeed, Mr. Boulton, who put up the money for the Watt steam engine, deserves to be known as the most important "industrial capitalist" who had lived up to that time.

Few people living today have ever given much thought to the truly spectacular properties of steam. It is widely viewed as just something coming out of a teakettle spout instead of what has been one of the most important work forces in civilization.

The steam produced from one cubic foot of water could expand to 1,600 cubic feet of vapor at atmospheric pressure. This represents 1,500 British Thermal Units (BTU's) or a potential useful energy total of 22 horsepower hours. If that cubic foot of water were boiled to vapor in one minute, it would produce 1,319 horsepower.

The power of steam engines had to be measured in units of work force, and the unit selected, "horsepower," was far from scientific. "Manpower" would have been more meaningful because it is the most important work power replaced by the engine.

One horsepower equals "33,000 foot pounds" per minute, meaning that it is enough to raise a weight of 33,000 pounds one foot every sixty seconds. Measured in time spans of sixty minutes, this becomes an almost unbelievable 1,980,000 pounds or about 2,000 tons per hour.

It boggles the mind to try to estimate the number of human workers that would be needed to provide the amount of energy equal to that in one horsepower. One approach would be to watch a steamshovel at work and compare the amount of dirt it can move with that moved by one man, using a hand shovel, in the same period of time. This would give us but a feeble appreciation for the tremendous multiplication of man's muscular productivity provided by the steam engine.

# THE TOOLS THAT MAKE
## ALL OTHER TOOLS

With steam power to drive them, man began to design and build complicated, sophisticated production tools that he previously only could have imagined. But before he could make these production tools, he needed a special group of tools known as machine tools. A machine tool is in effect a robot that replaces the work motions of a man's body, hands, and arms. The piece being worked on is held securely in the machine while a cutting tool travels over a pre-set path. There are several types of basic machine tools, each performing a specialized job of metalworking.

The following examples will show how machine tools were responsible for creating the age we live in.

James Watt had all the concepts worked out for his steam engine by 1765, but he could not build one that would work until John Wilkinson developed the world's first machine tool. The Wilkinson machine could bore a long, true, round hole in the cylinder accurate enough to hold the steam pressure required for Mr. Watt's engine. With this first machine tool of 1775, it became possible to have the first Watt steam engine operate in 1776.

Another class of machine tools, called turning lathes, were developed to make various sizes of round shafts and wheels. As early as 1700 there were small, hand-operated bench lathes employed to make the small shafts for clocks. By 1800, large power-driven lathes were in common use turning out the necessary pulleys and shafts for textile machinery, rollers required in steel making machinery, and creating the wheels of industry.

Richard Robert's planer, invented in 1817, was the machine tool that could cut broad, flat metal surfaces required for sliding bearings in such products as printing presses and locomotives.

The first operation in the sequence of making parts is to cut off a piece of metal of a desired size from bar stock. Metal cutting power saws were developed to cut identical pieces, one after another.

The power drill was an essential machine tool for drilling accurate holes as required in making almost any kind of machinery.

To machine the complex shapes required in the mechanism of

gun breeches and to mill teeth in gears, Eli Whitney invented the milling machine tool in 1818 that transformed this type of metalworking.

Since machine tool cutting is done by mechanical power and the machine operator does not have to physically guide the path of the tool while it cuts, these metalworking operations are done without muscle effort and without human error. This change in the concept of producing things repetitively without human effort was so revolutionary that the name "Industrial Revolution" was given to the age we live in.

Machine tools today are performing these same tasks plus ever-widening production operations.

On the following two pages you will see an illustrated chart of the transition from hand tools to basic metalworking machine tools. Vast improvements have been made, but these basic types of machine tools are employed in a modern machine shop. Although machine tools represent a relatively small part of industry, these machine tools must be credited with making the Industrial Revolution possible. They continue to make the basic units that are assembled into production implements and facilities that otherwise would remain merely ideas on the drawing board.

It was the machine tool industry that seized upon and forced improvement in the special steels that were first developed in the Iron Age. The goals were more speed, longer wear, and the ability to stand up under higher temperatures and pressures.

For example, in 1914, the Germans developed a new man-made metal called tungsten carbide that constituted a tremendous breakthrough. This new material was first used as the tips of metal cutting tools.

After Oliver Evans demonstrated "automation" with his mills that manufactured flour "untouched by human hands," the stage was set for development of machine tools that were needed to make the required manufacturing implements of production and transportation for an expanding number of products and services. The newest form of machine tooling is "numerical control," which has encouraged further steps in the improvement of automation. With this latest innovation, machine operations are controlled by programmed instructions recorded on tape.

What is next? No one knows for sure, but we can be confident that man's brain will never stop thinking about ways to improve and to use machine tools—the keys to all industrial production.

# THE HISTORY OF TOOLS IS THE

## STONE AGE

**DRILLING**

FLINT DRILLS

**CHOPPING**

POLISHED STONE CHISEL

POLISHED STONE AXE HEAD

**SLICING**

FLINT BLADES

**BURNISHING**

RUBBING STONE (used to sharpen tools)

**SCRAPING**

POLISHED STONE ADZE

**SAWING**

FLINT SAWS

**MEASURING**

DIGIT    PALM    CUBIT

## BRONZE AGE

BOW DRILL

BRONZE DRILL

BRONZE AXES

BRONZE KNIVES

RUBBING STONE    POUNDING BALL

BRONZE FILE

EGYPTIAN ADZE

BRONZE SCRAPING TOOLS

BRONZE SAWS

MASTER CUBIT STICK (Reference standard)

# HISTORY OF MAN'S PROGRESS

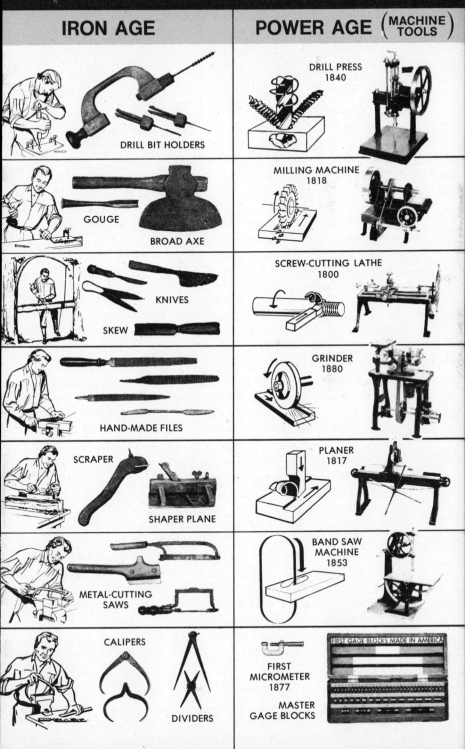

## IRON AGE

## POWER AGE ( MACHINE TOOLS )

DRILL BIT HOLDERS

DRILL PRESS
1840

GOUGE

BROAD AXE

MILLING MACHINE
1818

KNIVES

SKEW

SCREW-CUTTING LATHE
1800

HAND-MADE FILES

GRINDER
1880

SCRAPER

SHAPER PLANE

PLANER
1817

METAL-CUTTING
SAWS

BAND SAW
MACHINE
1853

CALIPERS

DIVIDERS

FIRST
MICROMETER
1877

MASTER
GAGE BLOCKS

FIRST GAGE BLOCKS MADE IN AMERICA

# ELI WHITNEY – THE FATHER
# OF MASS PRODUCTION

Until 1798, every device employing moving parts was made from start to finish by one craftsman who had to be skilled in every operation involved. Every part was individually processed and hand-fitted to its adjacent parts. This meant that the part dimensions of no two finished products were exactly the same.

Eli Whitney might not have been the first man to "think about" this, but the chances are that if the invention of his cotton gin had not turned out to be such a long, drawn out, exhausting, expensive patent fight (it took him 13 years to get a clear title) he would not have decided to go into the manufacture of firearms and put into practice his idea of making every corresponding musket part interchangeable.

Today, the rationale for interchangeable parts is obvious, but at the time it was a revolutionary break-through in manufacturing that set the pattern for mass production. Whitney's process involved his making a "master" musket, disassembling it and giving each individual part to different workmen, each of whom spent all his time making exact duplicates of that particular part. The concept of the "division of labor" was known to Adam Smith and other early economists, but without the corollary concept of interchangeable parts, could only be applied where dimensional differences did not matter—pins, for example.

The dramatic results were revealed one day when Whitney called upon representatives in the United States War Department. They complained that Whitney had not delivered a single musket on his government contract. His response was to show them a large table covered with loose parts. "Gentlemen," he said, "You are looking at ten unassembled muskets. And there are a thousand more. Every part fits every musket. If any gun needs repair, spare parts are immediately available." This demonstration impressed these officials, and Whitney went back to work, making thousands of muskets.

Whitney's achievement was not as easy as it sounds because to realize this first production venture, precision measurement had to be used.

Measuring is a science unto itself. It started in Egypt about

5,000 years ago with what was called the "Royal Cubit," which was the official standard of measuring. The Master Cubit was usually made of granite or diorite, substances that do not measurably expand or contract with changes in temperature. Anyone duplicating this measuring device in granite or wood was required periodically to have his working cubit checked against the original by the "Royal Master."

Every assembled mechanism has a measurement "tolerance," meaning an acceptable margin of error. In Whitney's time, it may have been 1/50th of an inch. Today, using precision gage blocks and light waves, accuracy can be controlled to millionths of an inch.

Whitney's standardization of parts made it possible to extend the previously known, but only broadly applied,"division of labor." Craftsmen making only one thing can become extraordinarily proficient, and can improve both the quantity and quality of their production with the added result of possibly lowering the product's cost and raising its value.

Someone else, at some later date, would undoubtedly have "thought up" Whitney's methods — in fact, a Frenchman named Leblanc and an American named Jeremy Bentham were known to have worked on the concept. But it was Eli Whitney who applied it, and the world can be grateful to the unscrupulous patent pirates, politicians, and legal manipulators who finally drove him out of the cotton gin business and into the musket business.

Thanks to Whitney, mass production was on its way.

# HOW POWER TOOLS
## CREATED THE FACTORY SYSTEM

In the early 1800's, conditions in the United States were ideal for the adoption of power tools. The new nation had enormous natural resources, a great labor shortage, and the personal freedom that fanned into a blaze the spark of ambition that is found in every heart. Before America's early settlers left their previous homelands, they were, by and large, ordinary individuals. Yet, they had several things in common—courage, the desire to be free, and the hope of improving their material welfare. These ordinary people from a diversity of cultural, social, political, and economic backgrounds were destined to become extraordinary.

It seemed providential that by the late 1700's, when America was ready to spread its economic wings, power tools were invented. These tools could compensate for America's greatest obstacle to economic progress—its shortage of labor. Horsepower was the magic multiplier of manpower, and it certainly came on the scene at exactly the right moment.

Power tools had two characteristics that forced change—they were too big to be used in the home, and they were too expensive to be owned by the workers using them. This forced the creation of special buildings called "mills" or "factories" to house the power tools. It also diverted a great deal of personal wealth into new investment channels—factory ownership—that were to become the essence of "capitalism."

These changes heralded a new type of economic life. The worker "came to work" every day to produce things decided upon by others, using tools belonging to others. His work was directed by a new group of men called managers who were responsible for deciding what goods would be produced and finding the customers willing and able to buy them.

Management was also charged with the responsibility of attracting the capital needed to run the factory and to make certain (or as certain as possible) that the payroll could be met. By common consent and legal precedent, the worker's wages had first claim on the income of the factory. This protection was an absolute social necessity for the success of the system.

The managers were seldom the outright owners of the factory, even though their personal fortunes might be invested. Huge amounts of money were needed to build the buildings and buy the machinery. Since few individuals could command the sums necessary, the money had to come from many people who bought "shares of stock" and became tool providers known as "stock-holders." In return for the use of their savings, they expected payments called "profits."

It is important to remember that these invested savings immediately took the form of tools, and that profit is really payment for the use of the tools.

# THE AMAZING RESPONSE
# OF MANY INTELLECTUALS TO
# THE INDUSTRIAL REVOLUTION

Along with the advent of the free enterprise factory system came a truly amazing and irrational crusade against it by many thought-leading intellectuals who professed the greatest humanitarian concern for the improvement of man's material welfare.

Starting in Europe and spreading to the United States, much of the philosophical and historical writing took dead aim at the morality and decency of the factory system, the private ownership of power tools, and their use for personal profit. While working conditions in the early stages of the Industrial Revolution were often harsh and strenuous, they were—contrary to romanticized portraits—in the main, no worse than those prevailing earlier. And, as onerous as they may appear to us and to these intellectuals, they brought overall improvement.

These intellectuals knew little about economics and had a lack of appreciation for the arithmetical proof of the first progress being made in the living standards of the common man in 2,000 years of history. They could not oppose increased productivity as such, but they could and did oppose private ownership and control. It is easy to understand how critics writing in the early stages of the Industrial Revolution could fear that it would only mean exploitation of the masses—they had little experience upon which to base their projections. It is, today, a continuing controversy, with many Marxian proponents leading the attack on private competitive enterprise. Their arguments are superficially attractive.

For the average man, "private property" conjures up images of immense individually held wealth, but remember that it also includes the holdings of vast numbers of the middle class—the backbone of private capitalism. If we abolish the first, we also throw out the second.

The dramatic progress of the twentieth century and the benefits this has brought to every segment of society has vindicated private capitalism. Yet, highly educated men, such as the group known as the New Left historians, are twisting economic principles and ignoring historical facts. Whatever their motives, they have failed to recognize and to present, in a fair and judicious manner, the benefits that they and millions of others have realized under free competitive enterprise in two hundred years of American history.

Free competitive enterprise is not fool-proof, and never will be, because free men are free to make mistakes. But, by any standard, it has produced the greatest good for the greatest number.

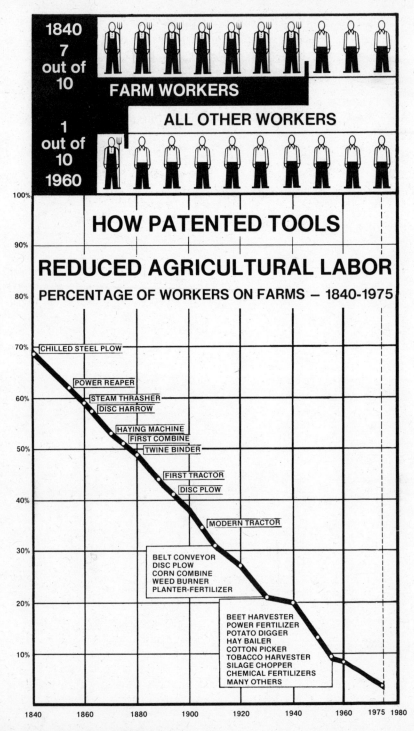

1840
7
out of
10

**FARM WORKERS**

**ALL OTHER WORKERS**

1
out of
10
1960

# HOW PATENTED TOOLS

# REDUCED AGRICULTURAL LABOR

## PERCENTAGE OF WORKERS ON FARMS — 1840-1975

CHILLED STEEL PLOW

POWER REAPER

STEAM THRASHER
DISC HARROW

HAYING MACHINE
FIRST COMBINE
TWINE BINDER

FIRST TRACTOR
DISC PLOW

MODERN TRACTOR

BELT CONVEYOR
DISC PLOW
CORN COMBINE
WEED BURNER
PLANTER-FERTILIZER

BEET HARVESTER
POWER FERTILIZER
POTATO DIGGER
HAY BAILER
COTTON PICKER
TOBACCO HARVESTER
SILAGE CHOPPER
CHEMICAL FERTILIZERS
MANY OTHERS

# THE IMPORTANCE OF PATENTS

Under free enterprise, the profit motive is the driving force behind economic progress, and patents help nurture the profit motive. Under the law, they give inventors 17 years exclusive use of their discoveries in which to try to profit from what they have added to engineering and production knowledge.

Most patented products are financial failures, but the chance of success keeps thousands of people doing what man has always needed to do—think up better tools, better products, and better ways to do things.

It would be impossible to demonstrate all the benefits that patents have contributed to man's material welfare, but it is practical to show what they have done for America in just one area—agriculture.

The "backwardness" of any nation can be measured by the percentage of its labor force still needed on the farm. Workers engaged in agriculture are not available for industrial, professional, or service jobs, which, as percentages of the labor force, are among the key indicators of economic and cultural progress.

On the facing page is conclusive evidence of how patented farm tools have freed millions of our people from back-breaking manual labor, while accounting for dramatic increases in the production of foods and fibers.

For the same reason some people are opposed to profits and to free enterprise, some are opposed to patents; they view patent royalties and corporate dividends as "unearned increments."

It is true that patents are designed to give an inventor a period of time, free from competition, in which to recoup his initial investment and perhaps realize a profit. But this temporary relief from competition is a small price for society to pay to stimulate the inventive power of its creative individual citizens—and it has paid off handsomely in an unparalleled outpouring of new ideas, new tools, and new products. Who among us would endure the harsh trials of an Eli Whitney, an Elias Howe, or a Samuel Morse without even the possibility of a future "pay day?"

If the people who would abolish patent royalties and profits would put them in proper perspective, they would see that what they propose would be a blow against man's material welfare.

# TRADE-MARKS –
# A SYMBOL OF QUALITY

When making a purchase, one of the first things the customer wants to know is: who made it? If his previous experience with a given brand was satisfactory, he can buy with confidence; if he is not familiar with the maker, he may take the recommendation of a person or organization whose judgement he trusts in making his decision whether or not to buy.

A good example of the customer's awareness of "who made it" was reported some years ago in the Soviet Union. Under state policy, all Russian shoe factories supposedly produced shoes of identical quality. But one of the factories produced superior shoes, and within a few months the public learned how to identify them by finding a distinguishing feature that served as a "trade-mark." It was only a tiny difference in the way the heels were sewn, but word-of-mouth was enough to cause customers to comb through a store's entire stock of shoes in search of the identifying stitch.

Trade-marks registered with the United States Patent Office give the holder sole use of that symbol. They are one of the major devices used by companies to establish recognition in the market place and to protect their reputation for quality. If those who produced inferior goods could freely use another company's trade-mark, the producer of inferior goods could damage that company's reputation and business. On the other hand, it is obvious that if a company's product quality is poor, the trade-mark may become a handicap to sales.

Trade-marks are essential to the operation of free enterprise. They make it possible to hold producers accountable for their performance and the quality of their products.

# ANOTHER INVENTION
# WHOSE TIME HAD COME

Had it not been for the "invention" of the limited liability corporation, the development and the expansion of the factory system undoubtedly would have been much slower, because it would have had to rely on different financial methods to raise capital to buy tools. Previous to the advent of the limited liability corporation, investors in a business that failed were held liable for their entire personal fortune. The "new" limited liability feature meant that the most an investor could lose was the amount he invested in the company. This feature did not reduce the risk of failure for any particular enterprise, but it opened the door for investors who were willing to risk a limited amount and, equally important, to a host of people who had very limited amounts of capital to invest.

At the same time, the public auction Stock Exchange (New York's being the largest) developed a ready market for the shares owned by investors who wanted to "get out," as well as a convenient selling service to those who wanted to "get in." This may sound unimportant, but without the Stock Market, the formulation and maintenance of capital would have been extremely difficult. The dual function of the Stock Exchange to service both the buyer and the seller through its member firms (who, in truth, are the Exchange) is what makes the wheels go 'round. It might be better understood if it were called the Tool Exchange because everything a corporation owns is used as a tool either for production or exchange. Recognizing this makes it easier to understand why profits on the use of invested money are really payments for the use of the tools.

American corporations have about 25,000,000 stockholders. The name stockholders is used synonymously with "shareowners."

# HOW THE UNITED STATES
# BECAME A GOOD CREDIT RISK

One basic reason why the British colonies in the New World succeeded where the French and Spanish failed was their degree of
self-determination and respect for private property rights. Every
British colony was originally financed by people who hoped to
make a profit. With no native population willing and able to work,
production was low, profits were disappointing, and the ownership soon reverted to the British Crown, which hoped to substitute
tax revenues for profits. But the Colonists' stubborn devotion to
economic freedom made excessive taxation impractical and
fanned the flames of the American Revolution.

With the end of a successful Revolution and the accompany-
ing peace came a fateful test of American character. The new nation had a $77 million war debt and was broke. Americans debated
whether the debt should be honored or repudiated. The decision
was enormously important because upon it hinged America's
credit rating with Europe where most of the available risk capital was concentrated.

Our European creditors did not really expect payment. But
it was Alexander Hamilton's exhortation to discharge this "obligation of national faith, honor, and reputation" that persuaded
the States to help provide the capital to pay the debt, which later
turned out to be both right and profitable. In 1805, the internal
investment potential of the United States was about $50 million.
Thanks to our new-found "reputation for honor," by 1837, more
than $200 million in European capital had been invested in the
United States. We were on our way to economic progress, and
by 1900, we achieved world industrial leadership.

One would think that since foreign capital is their primary
hope for rapid progress, this evidence that "honesty is the best
policy" would influence those underdeveloped nations that consistently repudiate, expropriate, or otherwise abuse foreign
capital.

# WHAT BETTER TOOLS
# DID FOR WAGES AND PRODUCTION

Between 1789 and 1860, power tools became the dominant influence in American manufacturing. With them came higher wages, shorter work days, and increased purchasing power. The reason, the only real reason, was greater output per worker.

Profits were high, but they benefited the worker because most of these profits were used to improve the tools with which the workers made their living. The technological changes in these years may not look impressive today, but in their time they called for an unprecedented outlay of capital when outside capital was scarce. So, reinvested earnings served a vital need at a vital time.

In the short run, the workers could have been paid higher wages at the expense of reinvested profits, but that also would have meant slower growth of the economy. With reinvested profits powering economic growth, the workers' wages increased dramatically over the long run. Between 1799 and 1859, per capita dollar income increased about 50% (to about $300) and purchasing power increased about 40%. Over the next 40 years, per capita income rose about 60%. By 1890, the workday had shrunk from 13 to 10 hours.

From 1849 to 1899, the number of factories increased from 123,025 (employing 957,059 wage earners) to 204,750 (employing 4,501,191). In that same period of time, total production wages increased from $236,755,000 to $1,892,574,000.

In one short century—a mere blink of history's eye—America had become the world's leading industrial nation.

# THE ABSOLUTE NECESSITY OF
# REPLACING INEFFICIENT TOOLS

In our intensely competitive world, military wars come and go, but trade wars are never-ending. Every nation wants to take customers away from every other nation.

In both kinds of wars, tools are a prime factor in determining the outcome. Armaments are the hardware of national security. Machine tools are the hardware of economic security. They are also the hardware of the war on poverty.

The United States became the world's leading industrial nation by investing in, maintaining, and replacing, as necessary, the largest stock of the most efficient power tools available. At one point, with only about 5% of the world's work force, we manufactured about 50% of the world's output. Our wages were the highest and our per unit labor costs were the lowest because the tools were doing as much as 95% of the work.

The driving force behind this progress was the personal profit incentive. There was no room for any tool, however good, if there was a better one to take its place.

Since World War II, this situation has changed. The best measurement of this change can be found in an examination of our stock of metal-cutting machines—the real "muscle" of manufacturing. Reliable data for this analysis comes from periodic surveys made by *American Machinist,* a leading trade magazine in the metalworking field. In October, 1973, this publication released its Eleventh International Inventory of Metalworking Equipment.

The national figures are alarming. In 1945, 62% of America's metal-cutting tools were under 10 years of age. By 1973, this proportion had dropped to 33% despite the fact that their useful productive lives had been drastically shortened by advancing technology. International comparisons are even more alarming. In Japan and Western Germany, the respective proportions of machine tools under 10 years old were about 63%. The Soviet Union showed 54%. Of the seven nations compared on this basis, the United States was from 5% to 30% behind other nations in its percentage of tools under 10 years old.

The reason for this situation is simple: the profits of American manufacturers have been too little (as low as 3¢ per dollar of sales) to finance significant investment in new tools. This coupled with inflation and inadequate depreciation allowances has made tool replacement enormously expensive. A simplified example: consider a 20-year old machine that cost $50,000. That is the amount that could be deducted from taxable income. Because of inflation, a new machine to replace it may well cost $100,000 today. The extra $50,000 needed must come from after-tax earnings. This means that an extra $100,000 must be earned, and 50% of it paid in taxes, in order to get the extra $50,000. As you can see, this makes the replacement of the $50,000 machine cost $150,000—three times the purchase price of the original machine.

It is difficult to focus public concern on this problem, because most people believe that net manufacturing profit per dollar of sales is more than 25¢. Were this true, prompt replacement of over-age tools would present no problem, and management would have no excuse for not doing it.

But as matters now stand, there is no substantial sympathetic understanding, governmental or private, of the formidable problem facing management. In fact, industry is under attack for making "too much profit."

Unless the problem of tool replacement is made easier through better earnings and/or realistic depreciation, the United States economy will continue to lose ground, and the economic security of its people—more jobs, better opportunities for every individual, and greater material welfare for everyone—will continue to be less secure.

# AUTOMOBILES – THE INDUSTRY
# THAT PUT IT ALL TOGETHER

In 1896, the public saw the first practical American-made automobile, a Duryea, chug around P. T. Barnum's circus ring. The first reaction was laughter. The second was: "who would ever want to own one?"

But quite a few people did want to own one, and courageous engineers rose to meet the challenge of producing them. From other industries the auto manufacturer could buy such items as wheels, engines, bodies, and axles. But they were not "fungible," meaning that they were not designed or engineered to work together. So every car was custom-built with hand-fitted, non-interchangeable parts. The market for autos was steady in spite of high costs. By 1900, sales rose to 4,192 cars.

R. E. Olds was the first man to attempt what was then considered "mass production," and his company was one of the handful that has survived the some 2,000 corporate failures. Another survivor was Henry Leland, who, as head of Cadillac, was one of the first to introduce Eli Whitney's concept of interchangeable parts to the automobile industry. But even in Leland's plant, there was inadequate division of labor. One man still assembled the entire car, running all over the plant to get the necessary parts.

A young engineer, Henry Ford, studied these methods, thought hard, and came up with a new idea—give each man only a few parts to install and bring the work to him on a conveyer belt. Simple? Yes, but also revolutionary. Thanks to Ford's new "assembly line," the number of engines assembled by 84 men doing 84 different jobs increased from 84 a day under the older approach to 352 per day under the new one. Thus an idea became an enormously important tool. Between 1908 and 1917, the time needed to assemble a Ford car dropped from 12 hours to 93 minutes. The price dropped about 50%, and Ford workers were paid twice as much for 8 hours of work as other auto workers could earn in 10 hours.

As Ford's competitors followed suit, the stage was set for the great expansion to meet the greatest public demand in history. America was to become the first, and at that time, only place in the world where automobile workers could afford to buy automobiles. The challenge for better, lower-cost components was taken up by hundreds of manufacturers, large and small, who thought up something to offer. Alfred P. Sloan contributed roller-bearings. Charles F. Kettering designed the first self-starter. Malcolm Loughead invented the hydraulic four-wheel brake system (Loughead's family later changed their name to Lockheed, which became synonymous with aviation). New production tools profliferated, and behind each one were the machine tools that make all other tools.

It is impossible to calculate what it would cost today to make a modern car with methods of the year 1900, paying current wages. The figure of $100,000 would probably be low. It is also impossible to evaluate the research and development and the risk capital that culminated in today's automobile. It is perhaps the greatest single achievement of free competitive enterprise.

The five major survivors of the intense competition are all big because bigness is essential to the auto business. Not counting imports, the public has its choice between approximately 325 distinct models of 58 model lines produced by the 5 major manufacturers and sold and serviced by some 25,000 dealers. In this industrial empire, the free customer is the true emperor.

# WHO SHARES THE INCOME
# FROM AUTOMOBILE PRODUCTION?

Automobile manufacturing provides a good example of who gets how much of the corporate income under free competitive enterprise. This is the story of what happened to $2,832 received for a typical car by a typical company from a typical dealer.

Everything manufactured has the same five basic costs. Below you will see the $2,832 broken down into these costs.

GOODS AND SERVICES BOUGHT OUTSIDE. . . . . . $1,351

This represents the small portion of total outside purchases made by the company chargeable to this particular car. This money paid for hundreds of things, went to hundreds of suppliers, who had to pay part of it to hundreds of their suppliers. Because payroll is about 90% of the cost of everything produced, it can be safely assumed that about $1,000 of this went into someone's paycheck, somewhere in the world.

DIRECT PAYROLLS AND BENEFITS. . . . . . . . . . . $ 945

The annual income of this company's employees at the time the car was produced averaged about $10,000. This $945 is that fraction of the manufacturer's payroll chargeable to this particular car. Some of this money was not immediately received by employees because it had to be payed into benefit and pension funds for their future benefit and security. In an analysis like this, one question is frequently raised: "How much of this payroll goes to top salaried officers?" The answer, in this case, is that 62 top directors and officers were paid about 1/100 of 1% for managing the production and sale of this car.

TAXES COLLECTED FOR GOVERNMENT. . . . . . . $ 256

This is the amount that the manufacturer had to collect from the customer on behalf of government. There is a legal "principle" that corporate taxes should not be passed on to the customer. The obvious truth is that there is no other place to get the money. Out of this $256, about $180 will become government payroll and much more will result when the balance is spent.

COST OF REPLACING WORN OUT TOOLS. . . . . . . $   87

This includes tools that are not yet physically worn out, but have become obsolete—too inefficient for competitive use—and must be discarded and replaced. Because of inflation, this $87 is not enough to buy the new tools, but it is all the tax-free "depreciation" that is presently allowed by government. Because old tools must be replaced, the extra money needed to purchase new tools must be taken out of the profit on which a 50% tax has already been paid. The money spent on new tools also creates payroll.

COST OF USING THE TOOLS (Profit). . . . . . . . . . . . $   193

Stockholders investment—tool money—is the backbone of the corporation and must be kept financially attractive. Profit is the amount paid by the customer for the use of the tools that produced his car. It must provide dividends and something left over for growth and survival. Of this $193, $95 was kept in the business and $98 was paid to stockholders in cash dividends.

Thus, we see what happened to the $2,832.

# AN IDEA THAT REVOLUTIONIZED
# FOOD SCIENCE

For thousands of years after man learned how to prepare food, he faced a troublesome problem—he had to eat it before it spoiled. Man learned how to salt and smoke food, but this changed the taste. He did not know that salting and smoking killed vitamins, but he knew something was unhealthy about it.

Since preserving food until it was ready to be consumed was a real problem, cities had to be near farms and grew no larger than the immediately available food supply permitted. Roads were bad and wagons were slow. On a long trip, travelers could not carry enough fresh food to reach their destination without replenishing their supplies along the way, which was chancy at best and frequently not possible.

About 1805, Emperor Napoleon Bonaparte, with an eye on the unreliability of foraging to feed troops on the march, offered a prize of 12,000 francs for a process that would preserve food for long periods of time. It was a candy maker named Nicholas Appert who conceived the idea that since it was the air that spoiled the food, the answer was to put it in air-tight containers. After encountering numerous roadblocks, he learned how to seal cooked food in glass jars with wax and wire. Bonaparte's government was impressed and tested this method by sending a batch of jars around the world on a ship to see if their contents would be preserved. They were, and in 1810, Appert received his 12,000 francs.

But glass jars had their drawbacks, so an Englishman named Peter Durand started experimenting with metal containers called "canisters." Because the iron had to be plated with tin, they became known simply as "tin cans." Durand had many production problems. For example, an expert worker could only make 6 cans per hour. But since glass jars were even more expensive than canisters, Durand's idea was commercially successful.

By 1850, canning was widely used; but it was not always successful—some of the food still spoiled. Another Frenchman, Louis Pasteur, thought that not air alone, but bacteria in the air spoiled food, and since heat kills bacteria, the problem could be solved by boiling the can with the food already sealed in.

Once Pasteur's theory proved true, the canning business came into its own, but it still involved slow, hard work. Around 1900, many toolmakers began to gear their efforts to improving the canning industry. Their progress was most impressive. One invention led to another. Arthur Sells designed a machine to remove corn from the cob; it handled 300 ears per minute. Another novel machine, which separated peas from the pod, did the work of 200 people. A salmon cleaner and cutter cleaned and cut 80 fish in a minute. A new high speed machine canned tomatoes untouched by human hands. With a pressure cooker, which took the human error out of canning, no one had to continuously check the temperature. Other machines filled and sealed cans. Conveyor belts speeded up the canning process, putting an end to carrying finished and unfinished canned goods around the plant by hand. Can production was increased from 40 to 400 cans per minute. Progress is still being made today—one relatively recent machine fills and seals 1,200 cans per minute.

The canning industry is another example of how man examines his laborious hand-production problems and conceives of better ways to do the work. This thinking is spurred by a fundamental human motivation—the profit motive. So is the resulting tool design, and the investment of risk capital needed to produce the tools. Non-profit economic systems can copy the technological progress of free enterprise nations, but there is little incentive for them to think about improving technology, and little chance that the government would approve investment in unproven innovations. Freedom of thought and action is the magic ingredient of progress in man's material welfare.

# WHAT TOOLS DID FOR TEXTILES

In almost every climate, man must have clothing. Along with food and shelter, it is necessary for survival. For untold centuries clothing was made from animal hides. Then man learned to interlace fibers to produce acceptable cloth, and for about 5,000 years, weaving was done by hand or on handlooms. Good cloth remained a luxury item, not because of the cost of the fiber, but because of the cost of the labor involved.

When power became available, men started to think about making a power loom. While illustrations of Egyptian looms date back to 2000 B.C., the design, construction, and use of these looms showed little significant improvement until the flying shuttle was designed by an Englishman, John Kay, in the early eighteenth century. Even when used on the handloom, it was a big improvement. On the power loom, the flying shuttle changed the whole approach to making cloth. An Englishman, Richard Arkwright, became famous for his textile machine inventions and his textile mills. The mass production of cotton cloth was so important to the English that their government passed laws prohibiting the export of the machines, blueprints, and the emigration of mechanical experts.

The art reached America only after young Samuel Slater, an apprentice, memorized the essential information and "slipped out of England." In 1790, he and two American partners started their own business. When Slater died in 1836, he was worth the then enormous sum of $635,000.

In 1813, Slater's innovations were followed by those of Frances Lowell, who, in Waltham, Massachusetts, erected the first factory to make cloth under one roof.

The success of Slater and Lowell drew competitors as honey draws bees, and the "cotton towns" of New England became the boom towns of the century. Unlike the later boom towns that lived or died on gold or silver deposits, these New England towns prospered and became well-run cities.

The eye-popping growth of textiles in the United States was a result of Yankee thrift, diligence, trading ability, and English trading restrictions. Everyone wanted and needed cotton cloth. It wore out at a predictable rate and had to be replaced. Cheap cotton cloth was one of the great contributions to man's welfare.

Every new automatic tool is, in the beginning, feared by workers who make the product by hand. Power looms were no exception. In 1589, at the behest of textile workers, Queen Elizabeth refused William Lee's request to patent his knitting machine. In France, hand laborers fearing unemployment, tossed wooden shoes (sabots, thus sabotage) into the machinery being used to produce clothing. Elias Howe demonstrated his sewing machine at the Quincy Hall Clothing Manufacturing Company in Boston in 1845, sewing five times as fast as the fastest seamstress. Expecting congratulations, Howe instead received abuse and criticism: some said it would throw thousands out of work, others that it was too costly.

Hostility toward better tools arises from ignorance regarding the potential size of markets. Lower prices and more uniform quality immediately expanded the textile market and the demand for textile workers.

A by-product of the burgeoning textile trade was the clothing factory made possible by plentiful low-cost cloth. The first American factory producing ready-to-wear garments was opened in 1830 in New Bedford, Massachusetts. At that time, this was a boon to sailors whose shore time was limited and to the Army in procuring uniforms. Today, it is a boon to millions.

Better tools always make things better for everyone. But fear of better tools always has hindered the progress of productivity.

# HOW THE GOODS GOT TO MARKET

An essential part of any efficient economy is transportation—water, rail, highway, and now air. Things are seldom found or produced in the places where they will be used or consumed. Young America lacked the capital needed to develop these essential economic tools. The first turnpikes were financed by businessmen using the corporate toll-road device. The first important turnpike, opened in 1794, ran 60 miles from Philadelphia to Lancaster, Pennsylvania. By 1800, seventy-two turnpike corporations had been formed.

But the big job of creating an efficient interstate network of connecting highways and canals could be done only by the Federal government, and here, again, capital was lacking. Thanks, however, to Alexander Hamilton, the United States had established a good credit rating in Europe, where most of the surplus capital was to be found. The $7,000,000 needed for the Erie Canal was raised on New York State bonds and came from London. It was such a financial success that overseas "canal" money became easy to borrow, and by 1880, the toll-canal system in the United States measured about 2,500 miles and carried approximately 20,000,000 tons of freight per year.

Railroads were slow getting started, largely because the individual states (from which charters had to be obtained) were heavily involved in toll-canal investments and did not want to foster competition.

But when the breakthrough came, it came quickly. Nine years after the Charleston and Hamburg railroad went into operation 3,000 miles of short-line railways had been built. Between 1840 and 1860, the figure grew to 31,000 miles.

But all did not go well with these railroads. Many were in the wrong places or were too close to other railroads to be profitable. It took 25 years to bring order and efficiency out of this haphazard growth, but in the meantime, business and the public benefited.

By 1870, the annual capital investment in railroads reached

$500,000,000, and by 1882, it had risen to $800,000,000. This all-important tool money came primarily from Europe and the by-now prosperous Eastern cities. But the time lag between financing and a profitable operation remained a formidable obstacle until the Federal government (and some states) granted the corporations free land on each side of the tracks and, in a few cases, second mortgage loans.

The "railroad barons" were not as ethical as they might have been, but they must be credited with determination and imagination. In 1870, Jay Cooke formed the first full-fledged "investment banking syndicate," involving 8 banking houses, to underwrite $2,000,000 of Pennsylvania Railroad bonds. Each firm guaranteed to find a market for their agreed percentage, even if they had to put up their own money.

Jay Cooke's "invention" of the syndicate was to become the pattern for investment banking by which billions of tool dollars flowed into private enterprise. The "invention" was not physical, but the results were. Here we see the familiar process of an idea turning into money, and the money turning into tools.

# ADVERTISING –
## AN ESSENTIAL MOVER OF GOODS

There are many kinds of advertising, all with a simple purpose — to acquaint the potential customer with products and services offered for sale and to persuade the prospect to buy them.

Advertising is one of the tools of production, because it helps insure a steady flow of orders and the volume of production necessary for steady employment and a profitable operation. Contrary to the opinion of many critics, advertising does not increase the price paid by the customer, and if successful, helps to reduce it. Mass production requires the mass markets created by advertising, while competition forces the cost savings of mass production to be reflected in lower prices.

Advertising has benefited tremendously from better tools. The performance of modern typesetting and printing equipment is spectacular.

The invention of radio and television put great pressure on purveyors of the printed word, and both the electronic and the print media have benefited from the competition. So have the buyers of advertising and the buyers of the advertised products.

Advertising is sometimes criticized as being dishonest. This occurs, of course, but the more an inferior product or fraudulent service is advertised, the sooner it disappears from the market.

Another charge leveled at advertising is that it tries to make people want things they do not really need. In the free market economy, this is the privilege of every enterprise. Who is to judge whether the free customer spends wisely?

Advertising is sometimes accused of exaggeration. In many cases this is true, but not really important. Every advertiser wants his product or service to be considered "best;" the public expects him to say so, and regards the superlatives as hyperbole rather than falsehood.

Advertising is a vital power booster in the transmission belt that moves the goods to the customers and helps complete the last step of production, the sale.

# RETAILING —
# THE LAST STEP OF PRODUCTION

The cost of retailing edible, durable, and non-durable goods is a critical factor in man's material welfare.

The oldest (and still used) method of getting food to the customer is the farmer's market—a public area to which farmers (and fishermen) bring their fresh produce and to which customers come to buy.

The oldest method of selling manufactured goods was peddling, making the peddler the original door-to-door salesman. Then came the "general store," which could sell goods for less than the peddler because the customer did the traveling. Also, the customer could have more confidence because, unlike the peddler, the store could be held accountable for quality. The general store was replaced in populated areas by the specialty store, which could buy its more limited line of goods in larger quantities and thus could afford to sell those goods for less than the general store.

These stores existed before the one-price policy, and the prices depended a great deal upon time-consuming haggling and dickering.

As transportation and postal service improved, mail-order houses appeared on the scene. Because their catalogs published prices, they created pressure for one-price policies in the stores they competed with for sales. The "price-tag" was a great labor-saving economic invention because it speeded up the purchasing process.

The next innovation was the department store, which could operate efficiently in urban centers. In effect, it combined the best features of the general store and of the specialty shop, namely, great variety and the savings effected by volume purchasing that could be passed on to the customer. By having so many things under one roof, they had the further strong advantage of saving shoppers time and trouble. Soon they began to offer delivery service, further strengthening their competitive position, and by the 1880's, the hard-pressed specialty stores were trying to get them regulated as monopolies.

The chain store—really a plan to syndicate managerial ability as well as to buy in quantity—was "invented" by 1900, but did not develop as rapidly as did department stores. The first successful chain was the Great Atlantic and Pacific Tea Company, which started by peddling door-to-door from wagons. When food chains arranged their goods so that the customers could serve themselves, they effected another substantial savings that could be passed on to the customers. Today, an efficient food chain can operate profitably on a net return of less than 2¢ per dollar of sales. The stern competition, the absolute necessity of advertising and posting prices, and the proximity of competing stores gives the customer great power.

Retailing has not directly benefited as much as other industries from improved tools. Aside from some mechanized stock handling and labor saving clerical equipment, the basic tools of retailing are still the sales floor and the display counter. The enormous increase in the values offered to customers over the years has resulted principally from the improved tools used in factories supplying the goods, with packaging presenting perhaps the most striking example.

Because department stores consider their operating costs a trade secret, it is difficult to determine the amount of profit made on any given purchase. But the following analysis of a single "luxury" item—a $110 woman's dress—is probably typical:

Cost of dress from manufacturer. . . . . . . . . . . . . . . . . . . $ 55.00
Cost of markdowns (special sales). . . . . . . . . . . . . . . . . . 11.00
Cost of theft and shortages. . . . . . . . . . . . . . . . . . . . . . 2.00
Wages, salaries, benefits. . . . . . . . . . . . . . . . . . . . . . . . 29.00
Overhead, sales promotion, etc.. . . . . . . . . . . . . . . . . . . . 2.00
Taxes. . . . . . . . . . . . . . . . . . . . . . . . . . . . . . . . . . . . . . 9.00
Profit. . . . . . . . . . . . . . . . . . . . . . . . . . . . . . . . . . . . . . 2.00
Collected from customer. . . . . . . . . . . . . . . . . . . . . . . . . $110.00

From this breakdown, which appeared in the New York Times, it appears that the profit margin of department stores is certainly not "excessive."

Retailing efficiency is a tribute to management ingenuity, and a triumph of free competition.

# THE EVOLUTION
# OF EXCHANGE

# EXCHANGE BEGAN WITH BARTER

Before money was invented, the exchange process was pure barter—goods for goods. This has been going on ever since man began to make more of something than he personally could use. So he bartered it for things made by other men who also had a surplus of some other goods.

Barter apparently started in the Stone Age because among the artifacts discovered in caves were tools made of rock not found anywhere near the location. By accident or intent, cavemen found other men who made something they wanted, and these other men were apparently willing to swap production.

Barter presupposes that both parties will benefit from the exchange. Both parties make a "profit" because the things they get are of more value to them than the things they give up. Even if this value is purely esthetic or based only on personal preference, the "profit motive" has to be present or the exchange will not be made.

With the development of shipping, barter became international trade, some of it hard-nosed product-for-product, some much more profitable because of personal preference values attached by others to such things as glass beads, trinkets, gaily colored cloth, tobacco, and rum.

We might call this sharp dealing or even cheating, but the fact remains that the people who got the trade goods were happy with them and were satisfied with what might appear to us to be "illusory profit." Viewed from the standpoint that gaudy clothing, jewelry, and trinkets were often symbols of power and status in particular cultures, the "profit" was very real to the recipients.

But barter was too clumsy a process to meet the evolving economic needs of exhange.

# WHY COMMODITY MONEY
# BECAME NECESSARY

The basic weakness of barter is that both parties have to want the other thing to be bartered at the same time. If a man wanted to trade some goats for some sheep, he had to find a sheep owner who wanted some goats right away. Even if the potential trading partners could agree on the ratio of exchange, the transaction could not take place unless there was also a coincidence of the need for each others' products.

Obviously, there was a great need for something of recognized value that could be safely held or stored against the time when the owner wanted to exchange it for something else. In other words, practical barter had no means of bridging the waiting time. Out of this deficiency came commodity money. During the history of man, many commodities have been used as money. All that is necessary is that they be durable, storeable, divisible, and of recognized value.

In early America, tobacco and beaver pelts, both having recognized value and being divisible into large or small quantities, were popular forms of commodity money that could be exchanged for almost anything. But people did not want to go around carrying tobacco or furs, so they left them in safe warehouses and used warehouse receipts in their transactions. In this function, these warehouses were banks where purchasing power was stored and protected.

Commodity money served an important purpose in expediting trade. In some ways gold and silver worked much better. But "trade goods" commodity money had a great stabilizing influence because, fraud aside, there were never more warehouse receipts in circulation than there were commodities in the warehouse.

# COMMERCIAL BANKING
# AND MONEY PROBLEMS

There was a basic similarity between the old "commodity ware-house" bank and the state-chartered commercial banks that fol-lowed: they both accepted commodity deposits and issued "money" in the form of receipts for these commodities. The criti-cal dissimilarity was that warehouse receipts did not exceed the actual furs, tobacco, and other products physically present. They were 100% redeemable at any time, that is, if everyone who held these receipts demanded them at the same time, there would be exactly enough commodities on hand to satisfy every receipt.

In contrast, the early state-chartered commercial banks in the United States, whose commodities (as established by the United States Constitution) were gold and silver, were forced to issue more receipts than the metal on hand. There simply was not enough precious metal to make every receipt redeemable. So, if they did not issue receipts in excess of the supply of these metals, there would not have been enough "money" to exchange the goods and services then existing and in production. Nor was this an innovation; in Europe, this had long been standard bank-ing practice.

Under "normal" conditions, this is safe because the private ownership of gold and silver produces no income. As a rule, when people know they can get the metal, they do not want it. But when they feel that they can sell the metal for more dollars than they paid for it — and thus make a profit — or fear for the sol-vency of the banks, the demand for redemption may exceed the supply, and if that happens, the banks are in trouble.

Between 1800 and 1857, the commercial banking system in the United States faltered five different times because of de-pression, wars, and other unanticipated events. At any given time, some banks were in trouble because of local events or poor judgement concerning how many extra "receipts" should be is-sued. In an attempt to stabilize the system, the Federal govern-ment passed the National Banking Act of 1863, which set stand-ards for operation and inspection of banks and offered incentives to state banks to become national banks. Most state banks joined up promptly, and the system improved markedly. But there were still too many bank notes in some places and not enough in others. So Congress, in 1914, created a network of 12 regional "banker's banks" known as the Federal Reserve System. Every national bank automatically became a "member" and deposited its reserves in the nearest Federal Reserve Bank. Each bank's paper money was called in and replaced by Federal Reserve notes. At that time, the new currency had to be backed by a minimum gold holding of 40% of the total outstanding certificates.

The "Fed" was a big improvement because it could shift money and credit to localities needing it most. The gold standard—which the United States first adopted in 1879 in a law that provided for the conversion of paper money into gold via reserve requirements—put a lid on the total amount that could be created. World War I and the ensuing post-war problems put enormous strains on the world economy, and these led many nations to abandon the gold standard. In 1933, the United States, also under monetary pressure, devalued the dollar and restricted the use of monetary gold to its transactions with the central banks of other countries. This devaluation boosted the dollar value of gold holdings by 67 per cent. To prevent United States citizens who held gold or gold certificates from realizing "windfall profits," the government outlawed the private ownership of gold and required that it be surrendered at the pre-devaluation price. In the early 1970's, the government eliminated gold reserve requirements for the banking system, thus effectively severing gold from the dollar except in transactions with other countries. Even though American citizens can now hold and own gold, they must buy it in the world gold markets and cannot directly convert their dollar holdings into gold by returning them to the monetary authorities. Consequently, paper money remains inconvertible.

# WHAT REALLY
# "BACKS" THE DOLLAR?

Redeemability in gold or silver makes any nation's money more desirable because if there are not enough "true economic goods" to balance the transactions, the metals are accepted in their place.

But there is a more basic asset that "backs" the value of any nation's money. It can be stated in one word—PRODUCTIVITY.

The worth of any nation's monetary unit hinges upon what can be purchased with it any any given point in time. That, in turn, hinges upon the nation's production of goods and services. Where productivity is high—when goods and services are produced with a minimum of time and effort—the value of the monetary unit is also normally high.

Rising living standards, the goal of every nation, demand an increase in the annual output of goods that exceeds the growth in population. There must be more goods and services per capita to satisfy that demand.

Clearly, then, the real "backing" for the United States dollar or any other nation's monetary unit lies in the nation's output of goods and services, and productivity is the key element in maintaining and increasing that output. In brief, if we produce less than we could, our dollar buys less than it should; if we produce more, it becomes worth more, so long as increases in the money supply are geared to increases in production.

Our productivity—output per manhour—determines whether our standard of living will rise, remain static, or decline, and new and better tools are the key to increases in productivity. This is true whether we consume these goods and services directly or use them in trade to obtain goods and services of other nations.

Monetarized gold and silver can help engender confidence in a nation's money, but without vigorous, growing production of useful goods, all the gold in the world would not "back" its currency. People cannot eat, wear, or sleep on or under gold. In times of severe famine people starve to death with gold in their pockets.

Confusing its huge stock of gold and silver with true economic "wealth" (instead of its domestic production of goods and services) was a major factor in the gradual process that tumbled Spain from its lofty perch as the world's wealthiest and most powerful nation in the fourteenth and fifteenth centuries.

The real source of any nation's wealth, high or low, lies in the production resulting from the combination of its labor, resources, and tools, and the total amount of that wealth, at any point in time, is determined by the productivity of its workers.

# THE IMPORTANCE OF
# DEPENDABLE MONEY

Ever since man was able to produce a surplus of whatever commodity he made, he ran into the problem of being unable to barter it immediately. He needed something he could store away until he was ready to exchange it. That something is money, and it has become the most necessary and most imperfect factor in man's economic life.

Aside from gold and silver, modern money is nothing more than numbers printed on pieces of paper and entries in the ledger books of financial institutions. We have no alternative but to use these numbers in measuring, evaluating, and exchanging the goods and services we produce.

In use, money is a receipt that we receive when we give something up (including our hours of labor) and that we use later when we decide to exchange it for something else.

The chief trouble with money has always been that there is no way of being sure of how much it will buy when it is spent. Man has always wanted his money to be a dependable store of value. The fact that it is not creates very difficult personal and corporate financial problems.

For example, when the individual saves for his old age, he cannot be sure that the amount he would need today will buy what he will need in the future. He cannot predict what his children's college education will cost, or what the purchasing power of his life insurance will be when it is cashed. In other words, he cannot plan with confidence.

The same holds true for businesses, which must plan years ahead for the financing of expansion programs. Even the relatively short time between the blueprint and the completed project is long enough in an inflationary era to make the original estimate fall far short.

Many factors contribute to the undependability of money as a store of value. A substantial part of the upward pressure on prices that erodes the value of monies stems from natural calamities, such as major crop failures and from changes in either the supply of particular goods and services or the demand for them—or both. As more of the world becomes industrialized, these factors become more critical, as witness the scramble by companies around the world for the resources needed to maintain or increase output. Moreover, many supplier countries have tried to increase their financial returns by setting higher prices on the raw materials under their control or by cutting back output, and thus, restricting the supply, which has the effect of boosting the prices of materials in strong demand. These higher raw materials costs result in upward pressure on prices for finished goods.

Another major cause of undependability of the monetary unit as a store of value is governmental action. In the United States and other countries, government decisions take the form of creating extra unearned money through the "printing press process" either to pay for wage rates in excess of productivity or to meet government expenses without raising taxes. The process used to be as direct as the name implies, the printing of greenbacks. The modern method, however, is far more subtle; to fund government operations, the government prints bonds that are accepted by commercial banks as collateral against checking accounts opened for the government. The banks do not lend the government any existing money, as would be the case if the government sold bonds directly to private citizens.

The process by which these extra dollars move into the national money supply is complicated, but two things can be said:

- These unearned dollars take on value by taking it away from earned money;
- They remain in the money supply indefinitely and function as interest-bearing greenbacks.

While the process may be complicated, the results are not: continued inflation and erosion of the purchasing power of the dollar.

# SOME CAUSES OF
# AND CURES FOR INFLATION

There are many causes of inflation. Some, such as droughts and widespread crop failures, are beyond man's ability to forecast, influence, or control. Normally, however, the inflationary effects of these are relatively short-lived, abating when the drought ends and the next crop comes in.

Other causes of inflation are man-made, and since they have a tendency to become "built into" the economy, their pernicious effects live on and on. These "inflation igniters" take many forms: international cartels that push the cost of petroleum and other basic materials to unwarranted levels; union policies that push wages up faster than productivity; inadequate investment in production tools that creates shortages and holds down productivity; and, fiscal and monetary policies that expand the money supply faster than output of goods and services.

That this nation's past fiscal policies have been inflationary can be readily documented. During the 1960's, the Administration of Lyndon B. Johnson chose to fund a war in Southeast Asia and huge "Great Society" programs at home without raising taxes enough to pay for them. Fearing domestic programs would be lost if higher taxes were imposed, President Johnson gambled that the war would be short, and with the end of the war, its drain on revenues would stop. But the war did not end, and the government continued to print money to pay its debts, the economy continued to overheat, and inflation continued and accelerated. This inflation proved to be a hidden, undeclared tax that eroded the purchasing power of earnings and of savings. Bonds, for example, lost half their purchasing power over the decade, dealing a severe blow to pension funds, colleges, and other institutions holding bonds, and to individuals living on their savings.

For all practical purposes, taxing savings and earnings via inflation became a de facto, undeclared public policy. Nor did the Administration of Richard M. Nixon reverse this de facto policy. Along with a Congress insensitive to or incapable of dealing with inflation, the Nixon Administration levied more of the same surreptitious tax, this time using it to "pay" for a redress in the nation's balance of payments as well as to sustain high defense and domestic program expenditures. The dollar devaluations were designed to make United States goods "more competitive" abroad, but they also had the effect of spurring inflation. First, these devaluations made foreign goods more costly in the United States, so they were inflationary in themselves. The second effect was much more damaging; by making, as intended, America's goods less expensive to others, they led directly to greatly increased purchases of our materials that contributed to widespread shortages and helped push domestic prices up dramatically. Inflation rates were already at peacetime highs for this nation well before the energy crisis, grain sales to Russia, crop failures, and dollar devaluations boosted them still further.

The hidden inflation tax has gone to support activities that past Administrations have been unwilling to try to fund through additional direct taxes. Taxes on current income are directly felt; taxing earnings and savings through inflation is not directly felt, and this is less dangerous politically. The issue is one of candor. If these programs are worth pursuing, they are worth paying for directly. We have the right and the duty to insist that government not do through a hidden tax what the people would not be willing to pay for through a direct tax. It is wrong to remain silent when so much that has been painfully built, so much that is precious to our traditions and our values, is being eroded by a continuing, unacknowledged capital levy.

Elsewhere in the book we have seen that wage increases in excess of productivity can only mean inflation. Obviously, if there are more claims on goods and services than there are goods and services, prices will rise. Yet, this is the precise effect of increases in compensation in excess of increases in productivity. This would not be possible without government cooperation in the expansion of the money supply, but since unemployment would result if the money supply did not increase to cover the unearned pay increases, that expansion has always occurred. The rise in productivity in this country in recent years has averaged about 3 per cent. That rise, whatever it is in a given year, sets the maximum overall increase in additional claims on goods that can be split up among workers, management, and investment in new capacity without contributing to inflation. Since payments for working overall account for about 90% of the total cost of doing business, it simply is not possible to grant broad increases in excess of productivity without fueling inflation.

Cartels and supplier combinations designed to increase returns on petroleum and other materials are harder for us to deal with because they involve problems that require international agreement and cooperation to solve. Certainly, high energy costs have spurred world inflation. Among some of the countries participating in such cartels, however, there is growing recognition that when they sow the winds of inflation, they as well as everyone else reap the whirlwind. Higher prices mean little if paper gains are offset by the erosion of purchasing power that stems from the inflation those higher prices generate.

Another cause of inflation is inadequate investment in the tools of production. The shortages that plagued the economy in recent years were basically not shortages of materials, but of the means of economically changing their place, shape, and form to make them usable. Had we had the capacity, we could have accommodated foreign demand without undue stress on domestic prices. The adequacy of our tools of production hinges upon the adequacy of profits and of depreciation allowances. During much of the past decade, these have not been sufficient to keep United States tools of production up-to-date. Since productivity increases real income, then obsolete, inadequate tools clearly will hold it down or decrease it.

The cures for inflation are relatively simple. Hold government spending to government income—balance the budget. Gear increases in the money supply to increases in the output of goods and services—to increases in productivity. Keep the rate of increases in labor compensation at or within the rate of increases in productivity. Modernize our tools of production so that we can increase our productivity and produce more with less cost and effort—it's the only way to increase real income.

# A HANDY TOOL FOR INFLATION WATCHERS:
## $M \times V = P \times Q$

Although it may not appear to at first glance, this formula, known as the Equation of Exchange, provides proof of an often stated truism—the selling price of the goods for sale equals the amount of money trying to buy them.

$M \times V$ means the number of dollars (M) in the spending stream multiplied by the speed (V) at which it is spent. For example, $10 million spent ("turned over") 10 times each year, buys $100 million in goods and service. $P \times Q$ is an equal amount arrived at by multiplying the number of things produced (Q) by their unit selling prices (P). For example, in an economy making nothing but widgets, $10 million turning over 10 times will buy a hundred million widgets priced at $1, fifty million priced at $2, and two hundred million priced at 50¢.

The total money or money value on one side of the equation is always equal to the total on the other. When there is a net change on one side, there must be a compensating change on the other side. Assuming that the above figures for our simplified example represent a "balanced economy," let us see what happens when something is changed. Suppose the customers slowed down their purchases and the money turned over only 5 times. This would cut spending in half. To balance this decline in turnover (V) without changing the money supply in circulation (M), one of three things would have to happen. Either (1) the price of widgets or (2) the number produced would be cut in half, and the total economy or gross national product would now be $50 million. The adjustment could, of course, be achieved through (3) a combination of changes in both price (P) and supply (Q), but in any event, the result would be the same—the equation would once again balance.

The process in the real world is, of course, more complicated, but it still follows this pattern.

Since any of the three basic adjustments would be bad for widget manufacturers, they would naturally try to do something about it. They could not speed up the turn-over (V), but they could go to Washington, D.C. (where money is created) and pressure the government to increase the money supply (M) by an amount equivalent to decline in turn-over (V). Thus, without changing production volume or selling prices, the equation would again balance at the original level, or at $100 million, everything else equal.

The big change would be in the purchasing power of the dollar. The monetary unit would now have only half of its former value. This is called currency inflation. If nothing else changed, this would be tolerable, but, as proved by history, other things would change. The people, worried about the future value of money, would step up the speed of spending, which would increase the multiplying power of V. But P $\times$ Q has to equal M $\times$ V, so something on the right hand side of the equation must change. We know what this will be, because, with money of lower per unit purchasing power, everyone producing and selling widgets must have more of it both to produce the widgets and to meet living expenses. So P has to go up until both sides balance. This is called price inflation.

If the process stopped here once the adjustment was made, it would be tolerable, but it seldom does. When and if government refuses to increase the M, unemployment will force down the P. But government dislikes unemployment, so it again increases the M, and again, and again.

Have you figured out which factor must be increased to stop this price spiral? It is, of course, the Q—the volume of production. It is the key factor, which, by increasing, makes it possible to increase the money supply, M, without raising the price level, P.

Obviously, increasing output (Q) requires increasing personal and overall productivity.

# WHY ALL COSTS ARE REALLY
# PAYMENTS FOR WORK

Economists have traditionally classified costs as payments for work, use of capital, and for rent. Were it possible, however, to properly analyze the components of national personal income, it would be found that this aggregate consists entirely of payments for working. The reason this analysis cannot be done definitively for any given year stems from the lag between the time some of the work is completed and the time payments for that work are made.

Wages and salaries are obviously payments for current work, and benefits can be current or delayed payments for work.

The income of the self-employed largely consists of payments for work, which may or may not be current work.

Dividends and interest are delayed payments for work previously completed to accumulate the property on which dividends and interest are paid.

Taxes are payments for the past and present work of government employees and of the people who produce the goods and services bought by government.

Rent is a delayed payment for the work done to accumulate the money needed to build the building or acquire other property for which rent is paid and current payment for maintenance and other work.

Retainers are current payments made in anticipation of work to be performed as specified by the agreements under which the payments are made.

Royalties on natural resources are delayed payments for the work done in discovering the resources that others extract or use.

Royalties on patents and copywrited written materials are delayed payments for the creative work involved.

These eight cost categories cover all of the real costs in any economy. The cost of such things as charity and public assistance are "transfer payments" of money earned by the work of others, which would be reflected in one of the eight basic cost categories.

The official figures for any year's national personal income show that about 83% of it constitutes immediate payments for working. The remaining 17%, traditionally termed "property payments," are largely delayed payments for working, even if received by the heirs of the people who did the work.

**PERSONAL INCOME IN THE U.S.**
**From working and from property**

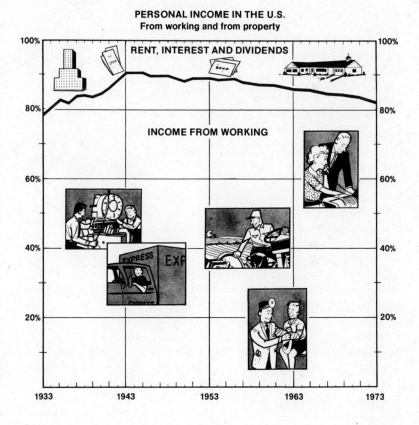

# MAN AS PRODUCER AND CUSTOMER

In the economic totality (See Page XVII) man has two functions. He is a producer of food, clothing, shelter, and thousands of other goods and services needed for a good life. He is also the customer who buys these things after they are produced.

As a producer, man wants to be paid all he can get. As a customer, he wants to pay as little as possible for what he buys. If he is a free worker, he can refuse to produce unless he is satisfied with the pay. If he is a free customer, he can refuse to buy unless he is satisfied with the price.

It is immediately obvious, therefore, that through his purchases he helps provide his own employment and payroll, and in the aggregate, if he refuses to purchase, he can put himself out of a job.

In the economic process, the total selling price always equals the total cost of production and exchange. To understand this, we must remember that the cost of taxes and profits are inescapably involved in the selling price.

This means that the amount of money needed to pay for the work done and the things produced passes into the hands of the customers. This also means that the amount of money changing hands is not important to the volume of goods and services changing hands. If we used seashells in place of dollars, the same exchanges would take place, providing each seashell had a mutually recognized value placed on it.

No economy is ever in perfect balance. There is always some underspending or overspending, but under normal conditions this does not result in enough imbalance to rock the boat. This imbalance has been well described as "unstable equilibrium," such as can be observed in the pendulum action of a clock.

Serious imbalance starts when, for one reason or another, the customers substantially reduce their spending or go on a buying spree through excessive use of credit. This destroys the rhythm of the production-consumption cycle. When purchases drop off, goods pile up and the people who would be busy replenishing the inventory become unemployed. These unemployed reduce their purchases and thus throw other people out of work in what amounts to a chain reaction.

A credit-based buying spree can have the opposite effect. As customers, people bid against one another for existing goods. This tends to raise prices, so, as producers, they demand and secure higher incomes. Unless these higher wages are justified by increases in productivity, these wage costs will further push up the already-high prices. If this is repeated long enough, the result is called a wage-price spiral, which can bring on runaway inflation.

The key point to remember is that, in the totality, whatever economic man may do, he does for or against his own welfare. He is two in one. He cannot separate his role as producer from that as customer.

# SOME CURRENT ECONOMIC CONSIDERATIONS

4

# THE EXTENT TO WHICH ECONOMICS
## IS A PREDICTABLE SCIENCE

Very few areas of knowledge can be accurately called exact sciences. The purely physical sciences such as chemistry, physics, and metallurgy are called exact sciences because within the limitations of the measuring devices or observation techniques used, every time the same things are done with the same components under the same conditions, the same results are obtained.

Medicine is a semi-exact science because, in many instances, the same treatments can be depended upon to produce the same results, but in other treatments the results are not certain. Many human physiological and psychological reactions are not uniformly predictable.

Economics is even a less exact science because the results of combining selected factors depends upon human action, which is as highly variable as any factor can be. If "x thousand" human beings were to state, with complete honesty, the economic actions they intended to take within the next month, and if economic predictions were to be based on those statements, the actual results would be wide of the mark. This is true even if the forecasts are based on group probabilities rather than on individual predictions, in spite of the fact that probabilities enable one to infer things about the behavior of a group that cannot be inferred about individual behavior.

Hundreds of changes could occur. For example, unpredictable weather conditions could cause higher food prices. Cartels controlling petroleum production can cause energy shortages. People planning a trip abroad could find themselves about to have a baby. New furniture could assume priority over a new car. Hospital bills could cancel out plans for home improvement. While some changes in individual plans will cancel each other out and, therefore, not affect the group forecast, other changes will be biased in one direction, causing the group forecast to fall short of or exceed original expectations. Economic planning is like trying to solve a mathematical equation involving an unknowable unknown factor.

To make economics even less of an exact science, the calculations are frequently subjected to political controls whose purpose is to guarantee that the unknown factor—namely, what the people are going to do—turns out to be the one that will make the government plan come true.

A simple example: in 1934, the United States government, desperate to raise depressed prices, injected what it thought would be stimulating deficit dollars into the national money supply. Theoretically, it looked as if it would work. Unfortunately for this plan, the people preferred to use the extra money to pay off some of their debts, reduce the mortgage, or put it in savings.

Economics is, however, an exact science to the degree that its operation can be expressed in exact formulas, charts, graphs, and diagrams. For example, the formula $MMW = NR + HE \times T$ is demonstrably true—the level of Man's Material Welfare does vary with the amount of Natural Resources, Human Energy, and "Tools" available to the economy and the way they are used. These factors both indicate the potential for growth and also set the limits upon that growth in any given time period. Since "Tools" represent the one factor that can be increased substantially within reasonable periods of time, analysis of the formula tells us that is the place to put great emphasis if we wish to increase Man's Material Welfare.

The Law of Supply and Demand is another case in point. In any monetary-based economy, prices will tend toward the intersection of supply and demand schedules—that is, toward the price at which the demand for a product matches the supply. Prices may be set by government fiat—and therefore not reflect this tendency—but if they are set too high and the need for the product is irresistible, the search for substitutes will be vigorously prosecuted until prices are corrected. If the need is not that strong, some goods will remain unpurchased. If, on the other hand, prices are set too low, shortages will result. Government-coerced or sponsored spending in the former instance and rationing and/or the "Black Market" in the latter may partially redress the imbalance, but they merely demonstrate how inferior this approach is to the unfettered mechanism of supply and demand in a free market. The Law of Supply and Demand can be temporarily ignored or tampered with, but its effects cannot be escaped.

In a free economy, most economic plans are made by private individuals and corporations. Very few are of national importance. Their success or failure affects relatively small groups of people. And, for everyone that is wrong, there are always others that are right. So the public does not dramatically suffer from the mistakes.

When economic plans are made by government, however, they usually operate on such a large scale that entire populations must share the failures.

# WHAT IS ECONOMIC FREEDOM?

Robinson Crusoe, on his fictitious island, had complete economic freedom, but it was not of his own choice, and relatively few men want such freedom.

All men are interdependent. Therefore, to be workable, economic freedom must be voluntarily restricted to insure their cooperation. A free economy is one in which men work for others, so that others will work for them. They give things up in order to get things.

But there are three basic freedoms that do not have to be given up, and in fact, cannot be given up if freedom is to have any meaning.

The first is the freedom of the worker to get as much as others are willing to give.

The second is the freedom of the owners of business to charge as much as customers are willing to pay.

The third is the freedom of the customer to pay as little as possible for the things he buys.

This can be likened to the principle of separation of powers, which is essential to democratic government. So, ideal economic freedom can only exist within a framework of voluntary compromise.

To the greatest possible degree, government should stay out of the act, except to function as the policeman, preventing unlawful acts and enforcing agreements freely reached between participants in the market place.

When properly practiced, this economic freedom creates many important other freedoms:

• The individual can train and apply for any job for which he believes he can qualify.

• Enterprise-minded individuals can save and invest in any legitimate business that excites their interest.

• They can produce whatever they think customers want and charge what they think customers are willing and able to pay.

- If successful, they can attract the investment of other's savings and become as "big" as the patronage of their customers permits.

This is the way prosperous free economies come into being. When government takes over, we see the other side of the coin:

- The worker's work is selected for him.
- The worker's wage is determined for him.
- Government decides what will be produced.
- Government decides how much things will cost.
- Private investment is replaced by bureaucratic allocation of tax money.

In the first steps of government planning, these conditions may not seem inevitable. Nevertheless, history shows that restrictions must be placed on every group because if any group is free to do as it pleases, the entire plan fails. In *The Gulag Archipelago*, Russian author Aleksandr I. Solzhenitsyn provides a chilling, contemporary account of how ruthless, illogical, and far-reaching implementation of these restrictions can be.

Freedom imposes a responsibility that people do not like—the need to think and decide. This is hard work, so the temptation to let government do it can be strong.

# WHY THERE WILL NEVER
# BE A "PERFECT ECONOMY"

The nature of man and the nature of his needs make a "perfect economy" impossible. There will always be "economic problems." It is possible to plan what the people could or should do, but there is no way of guaranteeing that they will do it.

Government force will not work. Throughout history, the many authoritarian efforts to control human action have been dismal failures. From ancient China to modern Russia, even the harshest penalties—including death—have not been effective in obtaining the kinds of total conformity they are adopted to achieve.

Not even the conscious, voluntary cooperation of free people can produce a perfectly balanced economy because the people, including corporations, cannot predict what they will have to do. Economic decisions are constantly being affected by changes and events beyond their control.

What then is the closest possible approach to a perfectly balanced economy? It is a policy of insuring that the free market forces of supply and demand operate without hindrance. That operation is like the anti-roll action of stabilizing fins mounted on the hulls of large vessels. The boat is always rolling one way or another, but it stays within limits controlled by back pressures that operate on the same self-correcting supply and demand principle mentioned above.

In the economy, when there is too much of something being produced, demand and, normally, prices fall off and production slows down until there is not enough of it to meet the demand. Then the cycle can start again. In this kind of self-correcting economy there are always hundreds of tiny "booms" and "busts," which stay tiny because they are quickly corrected by the voluntary actions of people and businesses affected. Most of them go virtually unnoticed in spite of the dynamic nature of the various sectors within the economy.

In any free economy, there is a steady flow of new products, new models, new ideas. These innovations succeed or fail depending upon the decision of the free customer to either accept or reject them. By buying or not buying, customers tell business that the idea is another small "boom" or "bust." The producer soon gets the message and either moves ahead, abandons the project, or makes changes in his planning and presentation.

In any economy, there is always either some unemployment or underemployment that can mean hardship. In a free economy, unemployment and underemployment stimulate the critics of private enterprise to lobby for the "repeal" of the natural law of supply and demand and to empower government bureaus to make the production decisions with the goal of achieving full-employment.

This can be a tempting proposal in times of trouble, but we should bear in mind the poor track record of government efforts in this direction.

There will always be mistakes. The difference is that when they are made by private business they are relatively small ones, but when they are made by government, they can be whoppers.

# HOW REAL IS COMPETITION
# UNDER FREE ENTERPRISE?

To understand the nature and extent of competition under free enterprise, let us imagine a company that is just about to begin operation. Not all of these situations would be true of any given company, but in the overall economy, they show the pattern:

1. The first requirement is for the prospective management to compete in the money market for the necessary capital.
2. When the news of the proposed new plant gets out, various towns and cities desiring additional payroll compete with each other to become the plant location. Many factors are involved: size and nature of available work force, transportation facilities, local taxes and tax concessions, health standards, recreational opportunities, educational facilities, police and fire protection, proximity of markets and of needed raw materials, availability of water, and similar relevant factors.
3. Next comes the competition among architects to design the plant, among contractors to build it, and among manufacturers and other suppliers to equip it.
4. Once the plant is finished, it must be staffed with people, mostly from within the immediate vicinity of the plant. This means that some members of the work force will have to be attracted from other local plants with competitive wage offers, better working conditions, or more desirable jobs.
5. It naturally follows that there will be competition among the new work force for the best jobs.
6. As the plant goes into production, there is competition among the suppliers of the needed materials and services.
7. When the products produced in the plant go to market, they must compete with those of other companies making the same thing and must offer the customers some inducement in the way of better price, quality, design, or service. If prices of similar products are the same or so close that it suggests price fixing or collusion, it must be remembered that all producers in most fields must pay about the same wages, the

same cost of materials, and the same taxes. With such similar costs, they inevitably have similar prices. The company might sell its products for less if (1) it is willing to forego some portion of the prospective profit while it is establishing a market for its goods, or (2) has developed a less expensive method of production. But in either case, the firms this company competes with will be forced to either adopt the same cost-saving production techniques, accept a lower profit margin, or try to wait it out in the hope that the new competitor has set prices too low to stay in business. In any of these events, the ultimate result would be the same: prices for comparable products will be very similar or even the same.

If the company's direct customers are not the ultimate consumer, that is, if the product is sold through distributors and/or dealers, additional arenas of competition are added. The distributors and/or dealers must compete with other distributors and/or dealers at their respective levels who sell similar products by offering better quality, better prices, or better service.

In a state-controlled economy, none of the above areas of competition would exist.

In this world of imperfect knowledge, there is no such thing as "perfect competition," since among other things this would require that all producers and all buyers have "perfect information" about all factors of production and about all other products. Moreover, there are "natural monopolies"—such as telephone, gas, and electric services—whose price structures are controlled by public service rate commissions, which may or may not judge wisely.

Nevertheless, "perfect competition," like truth, is an ideal to be pursued, and the knowledge that neither is ever likely to be achieved beyond question makes that pursuit no less worthwhile.

Competition in this country is real, it works—the world's highest standard of living attests to that—and no alternative to free competition has performed nearly as well.

# WHO SHOULD GET HOW MUCH
# FOR DOING WHAT?

The cost of human energy—the principal commodity necessary for production—would, in a completely free economy, naturally follow the Law of Supply and Demand without the distortion of monopolistic practices.

The "fairness" of any man's compensation would not be disputed because it would be set by the natural forces of the market place. If certain skills attract higher rewards because they are scarce relative to the demand, more people would be motivated to learn and to develop those skills and bring the supply into balance. This may occur quickly—a computer operator can be trained in a matter of weeks or months—or it may take years— it requires years of study and training to develop a competent computer systems analyst—but it always works.

This fact-of-life situation generally characterized the United States during the first 150 years of its economic life. By 1900, America became the world's most productive nation. It was the only place in the world where every person could realistically ask himself: "What do I want to be when I grow up?"

After 1900, a new force began to emerge that ultimately changed the way the market would determine wage levels. In 1914, the United States Congress passed the Clayton Anti-Trust Act, which exempted labor unions from the Sherman Anti-Trust Act of 1890, under which labor unions had been taken to court as monopolies.

In the early 1920's, the labor movement began to grow with membership reaching about 5 million workers. Then, the growth slowed, and after the Depression hit in 1929, union membership dropped to approximately 3 million. But even while membership was declining, a series of judicial decisions favorable to labor unions were made, including the United States Supreme Court decision of 1930 to uphold the Railway Labor Act of 1926, which established the legality of collective bargaining. Congress also acted, when in 1932, it passed the Norris-La Guardia Act, which made so-called "yellow dog" contracts invalid and virtually eliminated the use of court injunctions in labor disputes. The Wagner Act of 1935 stated bluntly that employees have the right of collective bargaining or other mutual aid or protection. This Act also established the National Labor Relations Board, giving the Board power to prevent "unfair labor practices." The stage was now set for dramatic growth of unions.

But an important question remained. It can be stated simply: which has precedence, the right of free entry into various occupations or the right to bargain collectively? If one "right" is exercised, the other cannot be. Stated another way, the issue is whether wage rates should be determined competitively or monopolistically.

While popularly regarded as counterpoises to enterprise monopoly, unions in fact serve mainly to buttress monopolies where they already exist and to help create them where they do not. This is equally true whether bargaining is conducted on a company-by-company or on an industry-wide basis. There is, however, an important difference between bargaining on a company-by-company basis and on an industry-wide level. In local collective bargaining, both labor and management must consider the impact of wage and benefit increases on the company's direct competition. This tends to exercise a strong moderating influence on both, and to make clear the need to gear increases in labor compensation to increases in productivity; otherwise they cannot be paid for because only moderate price increases, if any, could be passed on. The money must come from reduced costs and improved productivity. In local collective bargaining, other benefits of unions, including apprentice programs and administration of medical and pension funds for members, balance the restrictive effects of the union's monopoly power, and the overall effect of that power on competition is not strongly disruptive.

When, however, bargaining is conducted on an industry-wide basis, the situation changes completely. The moderating influence of concern about giving advantages to direct competitors is removed, since all competitors must pay the same wages and benefits. Thus management does not have to worry about its direct competition, and the union negotiators do not have to worry about immediate loss of jobs. In these circumstances, the industry as a whole passes on the necessary price increases to its customers, subject only to the effect that higher prices have on industry sales. For products in strong demand, that effect is relatively small, and therefore is not as effective a moderating influence as competition between industry member companies. What appears to be a struggle between management and labor over the division of corporate income in industry-wide bargaining really becomes a joint effort by both to extract higher prices from the industry's customers.

This means that wage increases won by unions—unless these increases do not exceed gains in productivity and do not trigger product price increases—come at the expense of unorganized workers, other members of the work force, and anyone else who has money to spend, not the companies involved.

Worse, union monopolies do the same things business monopolies do: waste resources and give economically undeserved rewards to the monopolists, which is why the Congress passed anti-trust laws to prevent business monopolies.

Since organized unions gain their wage increases largely at the expense of unorganized workers, the ultimate answer to widespread unionism could be complete unionism.

If every worker had the power to keep up with every other worker, the futility of inflationary, unearned wage raises—increases in excess of gains in productivity—would become so widely recognized that they probably would be abandoned by common consent.

# THE NECESSITY FOR
# INTELLIGENT COMPROMISE

Intelligent compromise in economic transactions is what makes the high production, prosperous, economic wheels go 'round.

It is the essence of the give-and-take process under which one man accepts less than he wants in exchange for the other fellow accepting less than he wants. This is called free bargaining and, obviously, cannot take place when either party can invoke the force of government on his side.

It naturally follows that if intelligent voluntary compromise cannot be reached and if the public welfare requires that the issue must be resolved and put into action, government has no choice but to establish procedures to resolve these disputes.

The operation of economic freedom, therefore, depends upon intelligent compromise between parties and the maintenance of good will and mutually beneficial cooperation.

This has always worked on balance in the United States in spite of the substantial advantages that are frequently enjoyed by one party or the other. The human quality called the spirit of fair play between free people usually comes to the rescue of deadlocked negotiations.

It is the practicality of depending upon this give-and-take solution that communist leaders and others not familiar with how our system works cannot understand. To them, the collapse of any free-bargaining, unregimented economy (which is how the communists view competitive private capitalism) is only a matter of time. They believe that economic freedom can only end in economic anarchy, as the weak become weaker and the strong use their power to destroy them. They contend that the Marxist way is better because the State settles all arguments before they can start, and the producers have no choice but to cooperate.

The proof of the pudding, however, is in the eating. Ever since 1918, the Soviet leaders have had absolute power to bring prosperity to their some 250,000,000 people. They have all of the manpower, natural resources, and arable land they could possibly need. They have had massive technological assistance, foreign aid, and access to the production techniques of the entire industrial world. Yet, their people have the lowest living standards of any population of the major industrial nations.

Two main things are obviously lacking:

- The freedom of the people to innovate, argue, and compromise;
- The freedom to produce more and keep a fair share for their own use.

The real cost of anything, the acid test of efficiency, can be measured in the hours of work needed to produce things. Every comparison of time-cost ever made between the U.S.A. and the U.S.S.R. has shown that the Soviets require about six to twenty times more man hours to produce their basic necessities.

Freedom does bring vigorous differences of opinion and hard-fought compromise, but it also brings high productivity and greater personal welfare.

# WHO PROFITS FROM PROFIT?

Profit is that part of the selling price collected on behalf of the stockholders and the Federal government.

When first collected, it is called "pre-tax profit," and becomes true profit after about half of it is paid in taxes. So, the first beneficiaries of profit are the people who work for government, the recipients of government pensions, benefit and relief payments, the people from whom the government buys goods and services, and those who receive the government's goods and services.

The second beneficiaries are the stockholders who, theoretically, receive all of the half that remains after taxes are paid. In practice, however, they receive only part of this in cash, the balance being retained in the business for "growth and survival." The retained profits benefit stockholders by increasing the value of their company, and the fact the company is making a profit helps attract additional investment capital.

The third beneficiaries are the company employees, who are assured of greater job and pension security and the ability of the company to maintain the stock of efficient tools upon which their productivity, their payroll, and future pay raises depend.

The fourth beneficiaries are all the people at large—everyone. Profits create investment, which creates tools, which create jobs that create other jobs, all of which create prosperity.

The other side of this coin is the absence of profits. This destroys the incentive to invest, forces the worker to use obsolete tools, forces government to find other sources of tax revenue, reduces productivity and payroll, increases unemployment, and decreases the supply of goods and services on which national prosperity depends.

In short, when the nation's businesses operate at reasonable levels of profit, the economic pie to be split up amongst the nation's citizens will be larger than when business as a whole operates at low or unprofitable levels. Stated another way, an additional 3% to 4% of after-tax manufacturing profit could spark the economy to an increase of anywhere from 10% to 20% annually; the Japanese, for example, by encouraging profitable businesses, recorded annual increases in output of 15% to 20% or more during the Sixties, and in turn, the material welfare of the Japanese people increased dramatically.

When Henry Ford doubled the wages of his workers in 1914, his competitors thought he was crazy. But he foresaw that if he voluntarily paid the extra wages he did not have to pay, his workers would outdo themselves (and also become customers), the company could sell more cars at lower prices, and ultimately, his enterprise would be far better off. He opted for a smaller percentage and was rewarded with a larger absolute return. Following the same reasoning, if government opted for a lower tax rate on corporate earnings, production would increase, the tax base would be larger, and the lower rate would produce more than the present revenue. And there would be more for everyone to share.

Directly or indirectly, everyone benefits from profits. Directly, everyone suffers from their absence. They are what makes competitive enterprise work. It is no accident that the word "profit" was derived from the word "progress;" they are inseparably linked.

# UNSOLVED
# PROBLEMS

# WILL THE MIDDLE CLASS
# SURVIVE PROGRESSIVE TAXATION?

The backbone of any democratic nation is its middle class. In fact, the emergence of a substantial number of modest-sized entrepreneurs is the first sign that an autocratic society (where there is only the economic top and bottom) is approaching democratic self-government. The development of a middle class normally takes a long time. In Europe, for example, the process took from 400 to 500 years and entailed the redevelopment of a viable monetary system, the revival of world trading and market places, and the freedom to make contracts and to participate in the formulation of the nation's political, social, and economic institutions. The transition from Feudal economies to modern commercial and industrial economies in Europe required a complete restructing of man's place in society and of his individual rights and responsibilities, and this process unfolded at different rates within specific nations. Nevertheless, as the various nations of Europe grew and prospered, so did their middle classes, and in fact, the growth and prosperity of individual nations could be gauged by the size and prosperity of their middle classes. By the time Great Britain, with its large middle class, became known as a "nation of shopkeepers" in the 1800's, it was the wealthiest and most powerful nation in the world.

The process, however, is reversible—the middle class also can be destroyed, and with it, the nation's economic vigor and well-being. This also normally takes a long time unless the destruction of the middle class occurs through war, revolution, or catastrophes such as the runaway inflation that occurred in the Weimar Republic in the 1920's and early 1930's, which helped set the stage for the ascendancy of Adolph Hitler and the Nazi Party. In the absence of such precipitating factors, the process can take the form of gradual confiscation of income and erosion of the property rights of the oncoming generation.

In general, this can be done in a variety of ways: retarding capital formation by imposing "progressive" income taxes; by taxing capital gains; and, through inheritance taxes, which prevent the passing on of accumulated personal wealth. All of these measures make it increasingly difficult for individuals to gather the capital necessary to launch or back the new business ventures that in the past helped the nation prosper and grow.

Few lawmakers who decide tax policy concern themselves with the destructive long-term impact of their decisions on the geese that lay America's golden eggs. Their responsibility is to collect taxes, and they naturally go where they think the revenue is to be found.

Steep progressive taxes are easy to "sell" to the public because they appear to be measures for "soaking the rich," an ever-popular appeal since "they can afford it." As attractive as it may sound, however, "soaking the rich" is a fallacy because it is always the middle class that gets "soaked." The "rich" are few in number. Progressive income taxes only affect current income, not wealth already accumulated, so income tax returns show who pays the bulk of progressive income taxes. The breakdown of individual tax returns for 1972, facing page, clearly shows that by far the bulk of tax dollars are extracted from those in the $5,000 - $25,000 income brackets. Moreover, the relatively few families with very large incomes are almost always well able to protect themselves with expensive lawyers and extensive charitable deductions. The middle class—those with incomes of $7,000 - $25,000 per year—represent about 35 million of the nation's estimated 54 million families. They are largely defenseless against the tax collector, and as a group, pay the bulk of the nation's income taxes.

Moreover, inflation "teams up" with the progressive income tax to reduce the real income of middle class wage earners; as individuals win inflated salary and wage increases, they move up into higher tax brackets. Not only do the dollars they receive buy less each year, but individuals must pay more of these dollars in taxes.

In some instances, the impact of the progressive income tax on individual tax-payers is all but incredible. For example, someone living or working in New York City must pay three income taxes: Federal, New York State, and New York City.

If all direct and indirect taxes paid by the middle class were taken into consideration, the average individual or family in this group probably hands over about 50% of his or its income to the government. Neither the very rich nor the lower income groups pay anything like that proportion of their income in

# Individual Income Tax Returns (1972)

Source: Internal Revenue Service
(*Money amounts in thousands of dollars)

| Size of Adjusted Gross Incomes | All Returns | Taxable Returns | | | | |
| --- | --- | --- | --- | --- | --- | --- |
| | | Number | Adjusted Gross Income* | Taxable Income* | Tax After Credit* | Average Tax |
| Total | 77,674,818 | 60,920,327 | $717,743,764 | $444,810,174 | $93,366,531 | $ 1,536 |
| No adjusted gross income | 433,606 | 1,561 | -155,366 | | | |
| $1 under $1,000 | 5,703,532 | 16,335 | 15,084 | 1,294 | 176 | 16 |
| $1,000 under $2,000 | 5,866,364 | 152,635 | 254,139 | 59,749 | 8,482 | 57 |
| $2,000 under $3,000 | 4,987,094 | 3,035,565 | 7,663,808 | 1,422,448 | 202,676 | 67 |
| $3,000 under $4,000 | 4,963,911 | 3,680,118 | 12,954,122 | 4,343,117 | 641,311 | 174 |
| $4,000 under $5,000 | 5,057,835 | 4,333,940 | 19,481,474 | 8,079,648 | 1,251,517 | 289 |
| $5,000 under $6,000 | 4,739,391 | 4,364,837 | 24,000,529 | 11,169,264 | 1,788,085 | 410 |
| $6,000 under $7,000 | 4,252,284 | 4,049,177 | 26,331,556 | 13,318,914 | 2,171,867 | 536 |
| $7,000 under $8,000 | 4,273,911 | 4,124,416 | 30,901,737 | 16,480,854 | 2,744,138 | 665 |
| $8,000 under $9,000 | 4,038,289 | 3,966,965 | 33,684,601 | 18,618,431 | 3,148,952 | 794 |
| $9,000 under $10,000 | 3,892,863 | 3,841,278 | 36,444,670 | 20,464,161 | 3,500,948 | 911 |
| $10,000 under $11,000 | 3,644,984 | 3,619,997 | 37,996,352 | 22,123,624 | 3,834,706 | 1,059 |
| $11,000 under $12,000 | 3,469,497 | 3,450,465 | 39,658,661 | 23,313,496 | 4,074,023 | 1,181 |
| $12,000 under $13,000 | 3,111,318 | 3,095,123 | 38,668,028 | 23,173,465 | 4,092,751 | 1,322 |
| $13,000 under $14,000 | 2,786,630 | 2,776,160 | 37,411,551 | 22,944,509 | 4,108,741 | 1,480 |
| $14,000 under $15,000 | 2,377,919 | 2,369,596 | 34,311,213 | 21,520,419 | 3,911,246 | 1,651 |
| $15,000 under $20,000 | 7,776,311 | 7,758,867 | 133,009,446 | 87,956,629 | 16,687,034 | 2,151 |
| $20,000 under $25,000 | 3,098,369 | 3,092,215 | 68,415,527 | 48,029,594 | 9,836,522 | 3,182 |
| $25,000 under $30,000 | 1,267,623 | 1,263,045 | 34,324,722 | 24,830,156 | 5,484,100 | 4,343 |
| $30,000 under $50,000 | 1,335,813 | 1,332,645 | 49,361,514 | 36,591,683 | 9,400,770 | 7,061 |
| $50,000 under $100,000 | 482,964 | 481,479 | 31,821,883 | 24,424,494 | 8,495,987 | 17,696 |
| $100,000 under $200,000 | 91,423 | 91,120 | 11,907,457 | 9,197,333 | 4,090,559 | 45,268 |
| $200,000 under $500,000 | 19,230 | 19,147 | 5,387,798 | 4,014,122 | 2,159,264 | 115,099 |
| $500,000 under $1,000,000 | 2,646 | 2,634 | 1,768,178 | 1,279,383 | 780,830 | 306,037 |
| $1,000,000 or more | 1,011 | 1,007 | 2,125,080 | 1,453,387 | 951,846 | 995,930 |

taxes, direct or indirect.

The long-range results of this policy may be observed in Great Britain today. The continuing growth of government control and activities, accompanied by the world's steepest progressive income taxes, has contributed to the dramatic erosion of Great Britain's economic and international strength and status. Great Britain is now at the point where she needs an economic miracle.

If present policies are pursued in the United States, we, too, will need a miracle to save our beleaguered middle class, which is absolutely essential to the continued strength and prosperity of the nation.

# WHAT IS A "FAIR"
## DISTRIBUTION OF INCOME?

In any economy, there will always be disputes as to what constitutes a "fair" distribution of income, whether opinions can be freely expressed or not. Everyone is entitled to his opinion concerning the value of the services performed by him and for him, but, obviously, his opinion is not the determining factor. If he happens to be in a position to force his opinion on others, he might try to do so, but very few people are in that position.

Under the Law of Supply and Demand, the free economy distributes economic rewards with no thought of "fairness" or "social justice." The free economy is a hard-boiled auction market: what do you have to offer, and how much are prospective customers willing to pay? The Law of Supply and Demand inexorably provides answers that come as close to social justice as man will ever reach.

Throughout economic history, however, men with special skills or in special groupings have quite often joined together in guilds, associations, and unions for the purpose of obtaining maximum economic rewards from society. To the extent that they are successful, the market for their services (which nevertheless follows the Law of Supply and Demand) does not operate as it would in the absence of their collective pressure. Group bargaining power becomes a special factor.

For the last decade in the United States, bargaining power of this type has been at an all-time high. So have the disputes concerning "fairness." Is a truck driver worth more than a schoolteacher? Is a garbage collector worth more than a stenographer? There is no use arguing individual cases, because everyone has his or her opinion of the true economic value of his or her skills.

There is, however, great value in investigations into the total economy because they disclose hard facts upon which opinions of "fairness" can be soundly based.

A much disputed issue is how payments for the use of property (rent, interest, and dividends) compare with payments for working. The United States Department of Commerce provides the facts. When all personal income is divided between payments for use of property and payments for work, it is found that since 1943, payments received for the use of property have averaged less than 15% of the total payments. In other words, payments for work are about 6-1/2 times as great as payments for the use of property. Bearing in mind the part that property plays in our material welfare, the reader can form his own opinion of "fairness."

An even sharper issue on which there is very little understanding is the division of corporate income between payroll and profit. Department of Commerce figures for firms other than financial institutions show that, during the past 10 years, the portion of the divisible income available for this purpose that went to payroll was about 10 times that of the portion that went to profits. Basically, profit is the amount collected from the customer for the use of the stockholders' tools, and payroll is the amount collected from the customer for the use of employees' human energy. In judging the "fairness" of this 10 to 1 ratio, the reader should bear in mind that tools, in most cases, provide well over 95% of the work energy.

Another fruitful area of investigation is the percentage of payroll paid to top executives, and the size of their "take-home" pay. In all cases, it is a tiny fraction of total revenue, and this percentage gets even smaller as the size of the companies examined gets bigger.

To paraphrase Josh Billings: the problem is not so much ignorance as it is people knowing things that aren't so.

# HAVE AMERICANS LOST THE
# WILL TO PRODUCE?

Every strong, democratic nation has been built on the careful, conscientious use of good tools of production. The people, as a whole, had the will and the desire to produce.

If, as many feel, the American people are losing their will to produce high quality, attractively priced goods, and to service them with a proper sense of responsibility, the United States will continue to lose ground and prestige in the competition for world economic leadership.

It will also suffer from chronic industrial unemployment because competition is no longer just national—almost every nation in the world has access to the American market—and the customer does not care where a high quality product was made.

One of the most startling pronouncements we have heard was included in a speech by the president of one of the large auto companies. He was quoted by the press as saying: "May the Good Lord spare me from buying one of our cars that was finished on a Monday."

The quality control dilemma management faces is more than just a discipline problem. Years ago, President John F. Kennedy put his finger on it when he called upon the nation to "return to the spirit of excellence."

Higher wages are not the answer; much of the least conscientious work is being done by the highest paid workers. In fact, affluence seems to be one of the biggest contributing factors. The will to produce is no longer spurred by the need to produce. The responsibility to produce is no longer a moral responsibility.

It is true that inadequate depreciation allowances and low-profit levels have slowed investment in new tools, as evidenced by the increasing age of American production equipment. This, in turn, has deprived us of the greater output potential newer equipment would provide. Nevertheless, tremendous increases in output—in productivity—would be realized if we worked harder at using what we have fully and efficiently.

The United States would not be the first great nation to be undermined by its own success. The more effortless prosperity becomes, the less the effort that is exerted. Noted elsewhere is historian Arnold Toynbee's observation that, at the time of their collapse, most of the great nations of the past were at the same state of moral decline now observed in America.

It is questionable whether even national economic disaster and hardship would restore the popular will to produce because it would probably be blamed, not on the quality of workmanship, but on the "System."

A promising course of action we can see is a determined public information campaign by management to regain the right to manage and "sell it" to workers and to the United States Congress. It is legal for unions to support (and often control) political candidates and incumbents. Management is fined, and even jailed, for making national political contributions, if the contributions are made from corporate funds.

The First Amendment gives management many rights that have not been effectively exercised. Some of these are natural rights—particularly the right of vigorous free speech—that have never been fully tested in the courts. Labor unions got where they are by frequently ignoring questions of the legality of what they wanted to do, and settling it later. At times, unions had to reverse themselves, but this approach gave them a tactical advantage. If management would really speak out and tell the union members, the investors, and the general public why low cost, high quality production is in everyone's long range interest, there could be a revolution in public opinion that would restore productive excellence to America.

And it would be a tremendous favor to both organized and unorganized workers.

# CAN WE SOLVE THE DILEMMA
# OF MASS EDUCATION?

A well-known educator has said: "When we started the task of educating everybody, we attempted the impossible. Having made the attempt, we now find it impossible to stop. We are not improving the quality of citizenship."

For thousands of years, children were educated (to the extent that they were) by their parents or, if they were rich, by tutors. In either case, it was individual education controlled by the person doing the teaching.

The Greeks had two contrasting theories about education. One assumed that the child had no knowledge except what it had been taught. The other contended that a vast store of knowledge lay latent in the human brain waiting to be stimulated into consciousness. This difference of opinion concerning theory and teaching methods still exists today between the "disiplined" school of thought and the "progressive" approach.

Educators do not even agree on the age at which schooling should start. Some say the third year. Others say the fourth year. Others say the seventh or eighth year. Still others say it depends on the child. There is considerable evidence that the late starters rapidly catch up with and often pass early starters. There is also considerable evidence that many parents want their child out from under their feet as soon as possible, and that many educators are only too happy to oblige.

In America, the tug-of-war between these two approaches moved from theory to practice as the states passed laws requiring compulsory education. Decisions had to be made. What should be taught? Who should teach it? How should the authority be divided between the teacher and the parent?

This involved broader questions concerning the purposes of education. Is it to prepare people to make a living? To teach morality? To induce patriotism? To establish respect for self-reliance and individual initiative?

In the early years of universal compulsory education in the United States, there was general agreement on the goals of education as set forth by two great educators, Horace Mann and

Williams Holmes McGuffey. The emphasis was on what children should be brought to believe in order to develop good character. Horace Mann summed up as follows: "Educate your children. Educate them in the great eternal principles of justice and right, which underline the entire length of human existence."

Mann provided the character-building philosophy, and McGuffey provided the text books. His Common School Readers were the dominate text books used in the classrooms. They consisted of excerpts from the world's greatest writers. While the child was learning to read, he, therefore, was being exposed to the thoughts of famous writers, philosophers, statesmen, and moralists. They were more than simply aids in the proper use of the English language; they did not avoid the "great issues" but dealt with them within the framework of moral and natural law. The student received a good elementary education and a set of beliefs as to what is right and wrong with emphasis on morality, industry, thrift, and personal responsibility.

The theories of Mann and McGuffey met their first true challenge from an educator named John Dewey who vigorously criticized the moral natural law viewpoint with the declaration that: "The aim of education should be to teach the child to think—not what to think."

Dewey did not believe in teaching that any "truth" is necessarily true. He believed that thinking should start with the examination of problems, not with the conclusions set forth by others, regardless of whom the others may be.

He went further and said that thought should aim not merely to understand the world but to influence and change it according to one's convictions.

Because, at this time, the rapid rise of new scientific knowledge was making a shambles of many previously accepted "facts," Dewey's premise that nothing is necessarily true concerning education was enthusiastically endorsed by many educators and textbook writers who were in basic disagreement with the Mann-McGuffey image of the most desirable citizen. If scientific theories were being revised, why not educational theories?

This appealed, at least to some extent, to all educators because it made their profession more influential. It appealed to many because it could make them the architects of a "brave new world" unhampered by the strictures of traditional American economic and social patterns of behavior. Needless to say, it appealed to most of the students when it was put into practice, because school usually became less work and more fun.

When the breakthrough came, it almost seemed as if the new textbooks had already been written and had been waiting to go to press. They came in an avalanche and soon were the dominant texts used in classroom instruction, particularly in the large public school systems. To the idealistic educator who sincerely sought a "better world," they were disappointing because many of these texts, particularly in the area of social science, were, and still are, devoted primarily to calling into question many of the tenets of the free enterprise profit system with little consideration of what would take its place.

Research and writing grants for the new "progressive" approach seemed to be plentiful. Conversely, the embattled "disciplined" or traditional approach received little support and even less favorable publicity. A few teachers, those most dedicated to the traditional approach, tried to stem the tide, which has not yet washed away the Mann and McGuffey approach but still threatens to.

That, in a nutshell, is what the frustrated parent who supports the traditional approach is up against. These parents believe that while a child should be encouraged to think, he or she should be provided a foundation on which to base his or her thinking. The power to determine which direction mass education shall take lies with those who write the textbooks and those who lobby for their adoption. Public education has become one of the nation's largest industries with a budget for primary, secondary, and higher education totaling more than $50 billion annually. As is true of many other huge enterprises, progressive education has developed its own momentum, and it is difficult to change the direction of that momentum but not impossible.

But the uneven results of the progressive/permissive system—which are being constantly recorded—are causing widespread reappraisals that might turn the tide.

# WHAT CONCERNED PARENTS CAN DO
# TO HELP EDUCATE THEIR CHILDREN

"As the twig is bent, so is the tree inclined."

It is now known that, in infants, attitudes and character traits begin forming at birth. Intelligence develops at a surprising rate. As has been recognized for centuries by the Jewish and Christian religions, a child of 12 has achieved his or her full reasoning potential and is considered capable of making responsible decisions. That is why Confirmation and Bar Mitzvah are set for that age.

By the age of 12, the individual's character and response "computer" has been pretty well programmed for life with his or her attitudes toward such things as personal honesty, responsibility, self-reliance, and respect for the property of others.

According to child psychologists, at the age of five, a child has begun to integrate into a social pattern all of the information and impressions he or she has picked up from observation, listening, looking at pictures, and simple reading. The child has convictions regarding what is "mine" and why, what is not "mine" and why, and what is "ours" and why. The thrust of these convictions are right or wrong depending upon what the child has previously been taught or not taught.

All of the foregoing suggest a way for concerned parents to influence the bending of the twig in what they consider the right direction. Through home guidance during infancy and the preschool and early grade school years, the child can be inoculated and immunized against the misleading economic and other "truths" to which he might be exposed in the classroom.

For those readers who might feel that economic attitudes are not formed this early in life, we quote from a 1961 study released by the Opinion Research Corporation of Princeton, New Jersey, which found that: "The child's view of the business world takes shape by the seventh grade and with a strong leaning toward big government."

This need not happen if parents do not want it to, because they can greatly influence most of what their children learn during the most important formative years. We must remember that this learning process goes on with or without parental guidance. It is a great, wide, wonderful world and the insatiable curiosity of the child's mind, which is much more intelligent and perceptive than generally considered, scoops up and absorbs huge quantities of impressions, experiences, and reactions. Good or bad, the learning process races on. Parents who take the easy path of "leaving that to the teacher" can become accessories to mis-education. Good character is formed in the home.

Admittedly, guided reading, close companionship, discriminating television viewing, and planned constructive "experiences" involving both parent and child are demanding and time consuming, but so is almost everything else worth doing.

There is a wealth of fascinating children's books and games waiting for parents who really want to help their children during the formative years. The minds of children are honest, open, and receptive to common sense. But after the magic age of twelve, attitudes, convictions, and opinions are very difficult to change, even in the light of contradictory evidence.

# THE FETISH OF "HIGHER EDUCATION"

The four-year liberal arts college curriculum was originally developed for young "gentlemen"—sons of well-to-do families—who, by and large, were destined to be ministers, lawyers, country gentlemen. Basically, the content was broad and philosophical and amounted to culture for culture's sake.

In affluent America, college has become a fetish and a status symbol. Nearly 50% of high school graduates go on to college.

As far back as 1950, Dr. Ben D. Wood, prominent Columbia University educational research authority, warned that: "At least half of the young people in college today do not really belong there. In return for four of the best years of their lives, about all they will get is a veneer of culture, most of it irrelevant to the task of becoming a productive, constructive member of our production and exchange economy."

About the same time, *Reader's Digest* published an article declaring: "Today's high school graduate plays a vital role in America's economic life that neither the college graduate nor the dropout can do as well."

The basic trouble is that we put too much emphasis on the value of a college education, whether it meets the requirements of a vocation or not. Unless a high school graduate is aiming at a profession or a field such as business administration where advanced study is desirable, he is ready to start his career. College often prolongs adolescence and delays development of the vital decision-making ability. After college, many youths are less prepared to "start" their careers than they were four years earlier.

One of the great fallacies of our time is that people stop learning when they leave school. Most high school graduates have acquired a basic knowledge of how the society functions and are ready to further develop the mental and physical skills that will help make their lives successful. Given the need and the opportunity, they are also much more able to cope with responsibility than most people believe. As a result, they are called upon to do much less than they could.

Business recognizes this, and most corporations recruit high school graduates for immediate employment. The knowledge they lack can be supplied by on-the-job training and special training courses, which can further their career in that particular industry.

But the college fetish is deeply rooted. As a spokesman for one large corporation put it: "We are spending more and more effort and money to recruit qualified high school graduates— and we are having a difficult time finding enough of them."

The needless parental sense of shame for not sending their son or daughter to college may persist for years, but there is a trend on the part of parents to leave the decision to the son or daughter. Even within the university community, there is a growing appreciation for the value of on-the-job experience, as reflected in the so-called "sabbatical year." Under this kind of program, the youth spends a year outside of the cocoon of education, using it to take a long look at the great, wide, wonderful world and what it has to offer. The idea is: "Do anything you want to. Try any job that appeals to you. Look at every opportunity in terms of what you would like your future to be."

These young people are not dropouts, they are "stop-outs," making up their own minds what they want to do. Those who continue college will know why and have a better idea of what they can expect it to do for them.

And those who do not continue also know why, and may be well started on a successful, happy career or vocation without losing any more time. Neither they nor their parents will feel any shame.

# HOW MUCH EDUCATION
## SHOULD BE VOCATIONAL?

Much of the snobbery that pervades higher education manifests itself in the undeserved second-class position assigned to vocational education and the jobs associated with it. The "ideal" curriculum in the minds of many is one built on "pure knowledge and culture" unrestricted by the practical problems of making a living.

Common sense tells us this is a much too limited concept. There is need for both untrammeled thinking and education geared to the demands of practical day-to-day activity. According to the psychologist, Hermann Ebbinghaus, the human mind will progressively forget information that is not reinforced by either repetition or practical use, and he even developed curves to show the rate of loss over time. Since society needs both thinkers and doers, strictly non-vocational education is a sure way to handicap or even waste a portion of one of our most precious natural resources: the performance of good minds capable of making practical, important contributions to the economy and to the material welfare of the people.

The goal of any constructive educational program is mature individuals capable of enjoying life and performing useful services. Through aptitude tests, psychologists can provide a strong indication of the kinds of things any given person is capable of doing well. This knowledge, if acted upon, can lead to personal success and satisfaction.

In most school systems, the most neglected educational area has been the vocational high school charged with teaching trades to students whose interests and capabilities lie in that direction. The budgets are usually low, teaching equipment often outdated, and the instruction uninspiring. This, too, has been a putdown for practical education.

Another handicap results from the artificially high status of liberal arts curriculums. Many students whose interests and aptitudes lean toward vocational work are encouraged to pursue liberal arts courses instead. Moreover, "problem" students often are shunted into vocational schools where, predictably, they do poorly. This, in turn, reinforces the "second rate" image of these schools. Nevertheless, when a student who has a real interest in learning a trade chooses a vocational curriculum, he is likely to learn more and perform better than he would in a strictly liberal arts curriculum, particularly, if the vocational courses are well presented.

Fortunately, the bias against vocational training has shown definite signs of abating in recent years. Some states have already upgraded these schools, improving the quality of instruction and modernizing the classroom machinery and equipment. In even the recent past, most vocational schools were behind the times; today, some states have even anticipated future employment trends and are teaching more than one trade to each student.

At the college level, the respectability of vocational training is being refurbished by the growing number of institutions dedicated to improving vocational training. These colleges, usually community-oriented, require that students select the vocation that they wish to pursue, be it salesmanship, business administration, nursing, shop work, office management, or similar career. The program works this way: for a given number of weeks, the students receive classroom instruction; then, for an equal length of time, they work in a business that is participating in the program, applying and expanding what they have learned. In most cases, they are hired as part-time employees and are paid for their work.

The enthusiastic, continuing cooperation and support by local business is proof that this plan is practical and that it works beautifully. These programs have a further advantage for both students and cooperating firms, since every participating employer carefully evaluates his student workers with an eye to possible full-time employment.

This type of education may not carry the social prestige of classic liberal arts, but it serves the badly needed purpose of giving ambitious young people a running start at a critically important stage of their professional careers.

# THE PUBLIC BENEFITS OF
# HIGHER EDUCATION FOR THE GIFTED

Genius, like gold, is where you find it. In America, where a person's background is less important than his qualifications, unusual talent generally shows up early because the educational system now provides equal opportunity for as much higher education as the gifted individual can absorb. Money, thanks to the scholarship system, is no longer the obstacle for most that it used to be.

Genius, although difficult to define and measure, is indispensable to the welfare of any nation, and its development deserves every reasonable subsidy required. In the arts, the professions, and the physical sciences, this has long been recognized. Only in the last 50 years, however, has there been proper recognition of the need to develop the ability to manage a business organization.

Outstanding managerial ability is probably just as rare as any other talent, and not much is known about early testing for aptitudes necessary to be a successful manager. But it is known that no free economy can be better than the quality of its business leadership. It is also known that this talent benefits tremendously from higher education. This is known because these benefits can be measured.

In May, 1974, *Fortune Magazine* published a revealing study of what the members of the 1949 senior class of one of the leading graduate business schools accomplished in their careers. In this arena, a good measurement of success is provided by arithmetic—dollar earnings.

In the year following graduation, the median income of this group was $5,000, indicating that most started their careers in relatively humble positions. In 1973, the median income was $53,561. Only 7% made less than $25,000. Only 5% made more than $200,000. A year after graduation, their median net worth was $3,846. In 1973, it was $250,980.

It is evident from the initial median net-worth figure that few members of the group were "born rich," and that most of these individuals made it on their own.

In 1973, their companies employed about 860,000 people and sold about $40 billion in goods and services. That is a sizeable chunk of the national economy.

The study indicates that most members of this graduating class do not consider themselves mental giants. When rating a choice of possible reasons for their success as "very helpful," only 59% mentioned "intelligence." "Motivation" was cited by 74%. The education they received in the Graduate School was listed by almost exactly the same percentage of the group as was motivation. "Personality" was selected as "very helpful" by a modest 47%, and only 7% mentioned "friendships."

It seems reasonable to conclude that the continued economic vigor of private enterprise depends upon motivating gifted people to become business managers. This raises an ominous question: to what extent are the pervasive, largely unanswered attacks on business—and the concomitant downgrading of management's contribution—eroding this motivation? We may not know until it is too late to do anything about it.

All of this points up a glaring omission in graduate business education: it teaches all about managing business, but very little about the philosophical underpinnings of, and necessity for, free competitive private enterprise. What is desperately needed for future management is a course in ideological debate—training in intellectual self-defense in the battle for favorable public opinion and political support.

# IS THIS THE WAVE OF OUR FUTURE?

In May, 1974, the Daniel Yankelovick opinion research organization released the findings of a significant poll designed to show the changing attitudes of college and non-college youth, and how these attitudes contrast. Some of the results are important indicators of the kind of society these young people are going to strive to bring about. And make no mistake, the future is in their hands.

Here are some of the most significant findings:

- In 1969, 79% of the non-college group believed that hard work always pays off. By 1973, this had dropped to 56%—a decline of 23%.
- In 1969, 56% of the college group believed that hard work always pays off. In 1973, it was 44%—a drop of 12%.
- In 1969, 60% of the non-college group believed in the importance of patriotism. By 1973, this had dropped to 40%—a decline of 20%.
- In 1969, 35% of the college group believed in the importance of patriotism. By 1973, this fell to 19%—a change of 16%.
- In 1969, 64% of the non-college group believed in the importance of religion. By 1973, this dropped sharply to 42%—a loss of 22%.
- In 1969, 38% of the college group believed in the importance of religion. By 1973, this had declined to 28%—a drop of 10%.
- In 1969, 57% of the non-college group disapproved of casual premarital sex. By 1973, this had dipped to 34%—a decline of 23%.
- In 1969, 34% of the college group disapproved of casual premarital sex. By 1973, this had fallen to 22%—a change of 12%.

One overall observation that can be made concerning these figures is that college and non-college attitudes, which until recently were very different, are moving closer together. The so-called "middle class morality," which used to be a buffer against radical change, seems to be disappearing.

The loss of "patriotism" is the only one that can be considered temporary. It was very difficult for many people to believe that the Korean and Vietnam Wars were efforts to stop the spread of communism through force, and as such, were steps taken in the long-range national defense. But this does not mean any direct attack on the United States would not promptly restore vigorous patriotism.

In contrast, the changed attitudes toward sexual customs and religion and the value of "hard work" are unlikely to be altered by dramatic events. These can be affected only by personal experience and individual, pragmatic evaluations of these lifestyles.

An immediate threat to the nation's material welfare is the bias against "big" business. Big business is indispensable to the efficient use of resources to meet the ever-changing needs of this growing and highly technological mass society. Popular demand for reformation or elimination of big business could be satisfied only by government intervention and control or outright ownership and operation. But even if this happened, the government would have to establish production units on the scale of big business, so nothing would really be changed in that respect. In effect, government control could mean the establishment of even more and even bigger big business.

The answer to this threat is clear—a massive dissemination of the basic facts concerning "big" corporations. Among these simple facts is the consideration that in a "big" economy, bigness is inevitable, essential, and highly desirable so long as fair, vigorous competition is assured.

# HOW FEDERAL FUNDS
# ARE COLLECTED AND SPENT

The popular demand for local uses of Federal funds stems from the fact that people know where these funds originate, and they want at least their "fair share" spent on projects and services from which they will directly benefit.

Most local, state, and Federal government revenues come from taxes, with the major exception being fees for licenses and other services. All taxes come from the production of the people. Every tax dollar starts as a local, indeed, an individual tax. So-called Federal funds are simply taxes collected from everyone, everywhere, and administered in Washington, D.C. The notion that the use of Federal funds for local purposes reduces the overall tax burden is really without foundation. Specific Congressional districts and states may receive more than their share of Federal funds, thereby reducing their tax burden, but only at the expense of other areas. This raises serious questions of equity.

Although every tax dollar collected starts as an individual tax, the form in which it is collected varies considerably. In a recent year, the Federal government collected approximately $260 billion. About $115 billion came from individual income taxes. About $40 billion was paid by corporations under the label of "corporate income tax;" since these monies are collected by these corporations as part of the selling price of their products, many economists view these monies as a "hidden sales tax" rather than an "income tax." About $68 billion was collected as Employment Taxes and Contributions, which was money that otherwise would have been retained by individuals—unless their state or local governments collected comparable taxes to produce the services that the Federal government provided with these tax revenues. About $17 billion came from Excise Taxes, another form of sales tax. The remaining $20 billion was collected from a variety of other sources.

Another source of Federal funds must be mentioned—deficit spending or the expenditure of dollars not collected as tax or other revenue but simply created via the "printing press" process and turned into checking accounts for government use. The same process of creating "unearned" dollars occurs when banks make private loans against mortgages and highly regarded promises "to pay."

In fact, this process is the basic mechanism by which the nation's money supply is expanded to meet the needs of the economy as it grows. To understand this, it is essential to understand the difference between borrowing from an individual and borrowing from a bank. If you borrow $100 from a friend, he either hands you the amount in cash or writes you a check, and the bank credits your account and debits his. In either case, you now have $100; he no longer does. No new money has been created. No inflation has taken place.

In contrast, when a commercial bank makes the loan, you have $100, but no one's account is debited; the money has simply been created, within the constraints of legal and bank lending policies. The money supply is immediately $100 larger. If you spend the $100 for goods, that amount of goods will normally be produced to maintain inventory. If you use the money to make something for sale, goods are produced. Even if you use it to pay off a debt, the recipient will use it in a way that stimulates production. The result, then, is that private borrowing indirectly or directly causes new goods and services to enter the private sector, helping to "soak up" the inflationary dollars created for your use. "Private inflation" lasts only until the dollars are balanced by new production. This could possibly be a substantial period of time, but the principle is clear: dollars are created, and they, in turn, cause goods and services to be created and placed on sale. The proceeds of the sale can be used to retire the loan. So, on balance, prudent private borrowing is self-liquidating, and to all practical purposes, is not inflationary.

In contrast, government borrowing based upon the same process of creating dollars can be strongly inflationary. Here's why.

While these funds also are used to create additional goods and services, a substantial portion of these (such as munitions, warships, tanks, and aircraft, etc.) are not placed on sale to help "soak up" the inflationary dollars created and paid out for their production. The net effect is to inject many more dollars into the hands of consumers than will be represented by additional consumer goods. Because the total price of goods on hand tends to equal the supply of spendable money, these dollars exert upward pressure on prices. Note that government spending financed by taxes does not have this effect. Tax monies used for government expenditures represent a transfer of claims for goods that already exist from individuals and corporations to the government, just as, in our example, the $100 loan from your friend transferred the money from him to you. No additional dollars are created.

That's why government should, as much as possible, limit its spending to its tax revenues and to borrowings from the existing money supply. These represent transfers; deficit borrowing by the government represents creation of additional funds without the benefit of the self-sustaining new money/new goods cycle that justifies its use in the private sector.

In summary, while the process of creating new money for the private sector and for the public sector are similar, the results are vastly different. Such new money created in the private sector is more or less tightly geared to the creation of additional consumer goods and services; it is not in the public sector.

If the Federal Reserve and the commercial banks do not properly regulate and administer the creation of new money, private "deficit" spending can be inflationary. In the public sector, it is virtually certain to be inflationary.

# WHY DEMOCRACY DOES NOT
# BREED STABLE MONEY

In any economy—particularly a dynamic, growing one—there will always be a certain amount of fluctuation in both the money supply and in prices.

The fluctuations occur as the population and the economy grow, as the supply of, or demand for, specific resources shift up and down, and as new processes are introduced. They also can be strongly affected by unusual major national or international developments, as were food prices by the foul weather that plagued crops worldwide in 1972. If, however, the increase in the money supply is geared to the increase in goods and services, the overall price trend will tend to be stable, major outside factors aside. That is, there will be little or no increase in, or "inflation" of, the overall price structure, and the monetary unit will retain most or all of its purchasing power from year to year, and under the right circumstances, could even increase it.

But democratic societies have a special problem that make this outcome unlikely. In a democracy, government is supposed to be responsive to the needs and desires of the people. Many of these needs and desires—including general government operations, defense, and social services—cost a great deal of money. When new services are added, the government should raise taxes to cover the extra cost. This would protect the value of the currency. But no one likes to pay taxes, and politicians are well aware of the fact that higher taxes could cause their constituents to vote them out of office.

So individual politicians have a difficult choice: raise taxes and increase the chances of political defeat, or create extra unearned money that takes on value only by diluting the value of all earned money. From the viewpoint of the politician, the ideal situation would be to be able to give things to the people without taking anything away from them. This ideal situation cannot be realized, but since taxes affect the individual directly while creating "unearned" money does not seem to, the path of least resistance is for the politician to create extra, unearned money.

This is a major reason why the history of currency in every

democratic nation has shown a steady though sometimes gradual decline in purchasing power. It seems to be an inevitable result of self-government.

If the people really understood the nature of money and taxes, they would not allow government to dilute their monetary unit. The starting point of this understanding is that taxes represent the goods and services that government needs to carry out its programs.

Centuries ago, the King's Cart would come around and actually take part of the people's produce. Unlike modern man, they turned over to government part of what they produced. In contrast, the tax-paying citizen of today is giving up claims on goods and services that he never really had in his possession. Therefore, it is not as readily apparent that the taxes each citizen pays are actually part of what he produces. This consideration is, in effect, buried in the complexities of the money system.

The most attractive aspect of the modern method of adding to the money supply ("borrowing" from the banking system) is that it seems to spare the people extra taxation. Actually, this process is the cruelest of all taxes because it hits the people twice: first, as the purchasing power of their money is reduced; second, when they have to pay the taxes needed to service the interest on the bonds issued for the "borrowing." Theoretically, there would be a third tax, the one needed to pay off the debt, but, in reality, there is no intention of ever paying it off. So the "borrowed" money becomes a permanent part of the money supply and the interest on it becomes part of the tax bill.

The reader might be wondering why the word "borrowing" is in quotation marks, and here the problem begins to get very complicated. This transaction is not borrowing in the accepted sense of the word. The government simply gives its I.O.U.'s to the bank, which in turn issues a checking balance to the government. As noted elsewhere, the bank does not have real (earned) money to lend for this purpose, but by adding the government I.O.U.'s to its real assets, the bank makes the transaction legal.

There is more to it than this—only a few experts completely understand the process—but the result is clearly evident; with the stroke of a pen, the bank has created new unearned money out of thin air. In their economic effect, these dollars are interest-bearing greenbacks.

This problem is presented not because there is a viable solution, but because informed public opinion might help hold the line in years to come.

# THE BASIC CONFLICT IN ECONOMIC THINKING — SHORT RANGE VERSUS LONG RANGE

There are two types of economic decisions. One is dictated by the immediate short-range benefits of a given action. The other is influenced by sober consideration and analysis of what is most beneficial for the long run.

Short-range planning is easier because it is based upon present trends and prospects for the immediate future. Long-range planning is more difficult because it requires more thought, there is more time for unexpected developments to upset the plan, and it also frequently involves sacrificing immediate benefits.

Everyone is forced to make these decisions at every level of their economic life. The choice between enjoying an expensive evening on the town or putting the money in the savings account may be relatively unimportant. But the choice between taking a trip to Europe or making a down payment on a house can be very important. So can the choice between spending available money or using it to get out of debt. The ultimate welfare of every family depends upon its accepting the discipline of long-range planning.

The same is true of nations. The present financial condition of the United States government is the result of some 40 years of short-range planning. We have long outlived the short-term benefits of government extravagance and monetary inflation and are now suffering the inevitable consequences. America has reached the point of trying to cure inflation with more inflation.

The adoption of long-range planning would involve so much temporary sacrifice and would be so politically unpopular that it seems all but beyond reach.

But it would be worth trying to achieve it.

# THE SIREN SONG OF
## "SCIENTIFIC" CENTRALIZED PLANNING

Whenever a free enterprise economy gets into serious trouble, the opponents of private business intensify their criticism, emphasizing a thesis that sounds very logical: a free economy has little integrated planning. Everyone does what they want to do within the framework of law, custom, and the availability of resources, so it is just a matter of time (so the argument goes) until this lack of direct planning and unbridled freedom of action turns into chaos. Suggested "solutions" include a variety of "fine tuning" approaches that theoretically would let business function much as it normally does, but which would extend incentives to business designed to encourage certain kinds of economic activity and discourage others.

An important drawback lies in the basic theoretical advantage of such planning—its potential for doing extensive good—since the other side of the coin is its capability of doing extensive harm if mistakes are made, and they will be. When a single company's plan fails, it generally affects only a tiny portion of the economy. In contrast, when government plans fail, the effects reverberate throughout the economy.

The quality of private decentralized planning is superior to public centralized planning because every one of the millions of private planners is affected directly by the results stemming from his decisions, and he bears the responsibility for his actions. He benefits or suffers depending upon the execution of the plans he helps develop as well as upon his experience, skill, and judgement. If his planning or execution is poor, the judgement of the market place is harsh and sure. But unsuccessful programs developed by government planners can continue as long as there are tax dollars available to cover the losses.

Freedom of individual economic action has always presented man with a problem. He wants it. He fights for it. Most of the time he enjoys it. But there are circumstances under which the exercise of freedom becomes a burden. In "hard" times, business and personal decision-making becomes difficult. This is when increased government intervention looks most attractive. This also is when it is most important for free men to maintain their faith in freedom and to keep their temporary hardships in proper perspective. Obviously, this is not easy. An examination of history shows that freedom is much more likely to be voluntarily surrendered than seized by force.

This surrender has frequently come in gradual stages. The situation in the United States can be measured by the steady growth of the Public Sector, meaning the economic activities undertaken, directed, or controlled by government. The change-over from private to public control of any given economic activity means that it is moved out of the competitive area in which good management is a condition of survival, and into a nebulous area where performance and service to the general welfare is difficult to measure.

# THE "TRADE-OFFS" ASSOCIATED
# WITH THE MINIMUM WAGE

Every economic action has consequences in both interrelated and in apparently unrelated, and thus unexpected areas. Nothing in our economy exists in a vacuum. Changes should be, but seldom are, made in light of what else is going to change, or in the jargon of the systems analyst, "following careful analysis of the probable trade-offs."

A case in point is the notion that government, by legislating higher minimum wages, can increase the welfare of the lowest paid echelon of employees. The goal is laudable and even works for some individuals in the short run, but then the "trade-offs" begin popping up.

These increases have three immediate results. First, those employees previously below the minimum whose work is worth the higher wage have more dollars to spend. Second, the marginal workers who are unable to contribute enough to earn the new minimum wage are fired. Third is the upward impact on other wages or what has been called the "ripple effect." Workers in the second lowest echelon, formerly contented with what has now become the minimum, demand an "equitable" increase and usually get it. The next echelon is stimulated to follow suit, and the impact may not stop until it reaches the top.

In an economy not dedicated to full employment, this could not happen because there would not be enough money to meet the payroll. But in the United States, the dollar shortage can be circumvented by simply inflating the currency.

If this extra payroll is not offset by increased production, the inevitable result is higher prices that cancel out the hoped-for increase in purchasing power. So the final scene in this scenario puts the intended beneficiaries (those who are able to hold their jobs) back where they started. With two exceptions, no group is better or worse off on balance than they were before the raise. They are just handling more money. The groups that are worse off are first, those who are fired, and second, the retired, handicapped, and other individuals living on fixed incomes and those whose incomes do not keep pace with the rate of inflation. The reduction in their purchasing power is automatic and inexorable.

# THE PROS AND CONS
# OF FOREIGN AID

The United States is spending too much money on foreign aid in terms of the objectives it hopes to realize. These objectives include: world peace; free trade; independence and freedom for every nation; and, improvement in man's material welfare.

In some instances, foreign aid was clearly in America's best interest as exemplified by the highly successful Marshall Plan to relieve the devastation of Europe in the wake of World War II. The physical, political, social, and economic chaos that was Europe was aptly described by Sir Winston Churchill as: "a rubble heap, a breeding ground for pestilence and hatred." Senator Arthur H. Vandenburg of Michigan, when championing the Marshall Plan, contended the "grim truth" is that America's self-interest, economy, and security are inseverably linked with the objectives of individual liberty, free institutions, and genuine independence. Perhaps because of these objectives, the Soviet Union condemned and opposed the Marshall Plan.

But not all United States foreign aid has been so successful. In Latin America, for example, the United States has spent millions of dollars for economic improvement programs, but these have been frustrated by the population explosion and misuse of the funds by local governments.

Southeast Asia is still a battleground in spite of the billions of United States dollars in economic and military assistance, and even more important, the sacrifice of over 50 thousand American lives. Japan, which received extensive United States financial and technical post-war assistance provides an example of mixed results. On the one hand, she is a valued trading partner, while on the other hand, she discriminates against many American goods by throwing up restrictive import and investment barriers.

Foreign aid is frequently criticized at times when the government programs can be financed only through increasing the national debt, inflating the currency, and raising the peoples' cost of living.

The best form of foreign aid is mutually profitable foreign trade. On balance, this helps everyone and generally penalizes no one as long as every nation has something to trade. But to get this kind of trade, we must be as good at trading as the people we are trading with.

There are many ways of disguising unfair trade practices, including tariffs, import licences, exchange rates, quotas, and export subsidies that are too complicated for most of us to understand. Those nations that have gained entry into the lucrative American market are going to lobby aggressively to keep any unfair advantages they may enjoy.

We live in a tough, hungry world, with each nation looking out for its own best interest.

As a participant in international trade, America must revitalize the old "Yankee Trader" tradition. Since all Americans have a stake in international trade, each of us, whether in business, labor, or government, should work together for a fair, balanced, and realistic exchange of what we have for what other nations have.

The United States does not owe other nations anything but honest trading on an equitable quid pro quo basis. What we choose to give away has many names, but it should not be confused with trade.

# IS REAL TAX REFORM POSSIBLE?

Most tax experts agree that present tax laws are difficult to reform, tangled as they are in political, sociological, and economic considerations. Every effort to simplify them seems to bring additional questions and complications.

The only answer—if it even is an answer—is to throw them out and start over. This solution, in principle, is easy to sell but always raises the questions: "start over with what and where?" It would not be enough for any new Federal plan to be economically practical; it would also have to be politically practical, and satisfy the conflicting interests that exist among major groups.

There is one approach that just might make it. The original idea must be credited to Wadsworth W. Mount of Warren, New Jersey, an authority on taxes. Here is his train of thought in condensed form:

1. All taxes are made possible by the income from production.
2. The selling price, except for taxes, is the total of the value added by business during each step of production.
3. Business is a highly efficient tax collector because the tax becomes part of the selling price.
4. Using "value added" as a base, business could collect virtually all Federal taxes. Since value added is the difference between external cost and the amount received from customers, every business already keeps such a record.
5. The rate of taxation could vary with the needs of government.

Mount's plan, first proposed in 1941, should not be confused with the "value added tax" adopted by European Common Market nations. These loose applications of the idea involve exemptions and exceptions, defeating the efficiency of an "across-the-board" tax. It also causes an increase in the cost of collection and compliance.

The Mount plan would eliminate the need for Federal income taxes. It would be self-enforcing and virtually cheat-proof. It would reach the entire Gross National Product. As a tax base, it would be far more stable than profit and other forms of income and would eliminate the gross inequities traceable to the maze of today's Federal tax laws.

Best of all, it might be politically acceptable.

# THE GOOD AND BAD
# OF ORGANIZED LABOR

We cannot think of any socio-economic institution that is or was all good or all bad. While "labor societies" in America date back to the seventeenth century, the first effective national labor movement in the United States actually began under the leadership of Samuel P. Gompers, who in 1881, helped to form a confederation of trades that later became the American Federation of Labor. The image of the American labor movement was later badly damaged by the association with it of such avowed enemies of private capitalism as Eugene V. Debs, William Haywood, and Daniel De Leon, the last named being the author of the incredible assertion: "profit is bigger than payroll." This demonstrably false contention is still accepted as truth by many people. The radical leaders of the Industrial Workers of the World (IWW) aroused a degree of suspicion, hatred, and opposition on the part of management and owners that lasted for decades and still colors company relations with other labor groups.

But much good was to come from labor unions. Beginning in the early 1800's, unions worked for such goals as shorter work days and universal free education, both of which are now taken for granted. Also, when David Dubinsky's International Ladies Garment Workers struck the manufacturers, the strike was really directed against the low prices paid by the industry's customers. When these customers found that all their sources of supply were forced to pay higher wages, and consequently, had to charge higher prices or shut down, the buyer's hammerlock was broken. The shamefully low "sweatshop" wages were raised, as were the inadequate industry profits. Management learned much from constructive labor unions and most of it benefited business.

Gompers made a big contribution when he declared in a speech at a Federation meeting in 1912 that: "The worst crime against working people is a company that fails to make a profit." Unfortunately, many employers missed this opportunity to improve their employee relations by not revealing their profit and loss positions because they considered these "no business of the unions."

Without question, labor unions have been responsible for a large part of the nation's economic progress and productivity. For example, when union pressure resulted in improved wages and working conditions in one plant, the non-unionized plant next door had to either follow suit or risk losing good employees. Very often, improved working conditions and shorter hours substantially boosted productivity, improved quality, and reduced scrap and rejects.

John L. Lewis of the United Mine Workers was rough and tough with a program that worked—fewer coal-mining jobs, better tools, better pay. And he barked to his members: "You got your raise. Now, be sure you earn it."

What might now be called punitive union action (against both the employer and the public) did not really start until after Congress legalized industry-wide collective bargaining, and until government employees, who were supposedly not legally allowed to strike, found ways to exercise their monopoly power.

Today, work in the private sector of the economy and most public services can be interrupted by a small number of national unions.

For a long time, labor did not have enough legal power. Now many people feel it has too much, not only for the good of the nation, but for its own good as well.

# WHAT ARE THE SOCIAL
# RESPONSIBILITIES OF BUSINESS?

There is a general impression in the public mind that corporations can easily assume the cost of necessary or desirable social and ecological programs in the communities where their plants are located without financial strain or higher selling prices. This presents a problem that will be with us for a long time and needs basic understanding.

Let us start with the prime responsibilities of the average corporation. First, it must attract needed capital and keep the stockholders satisfied with the return on their investment. Second, it must pay high enough wages to attract and hold qualified employees. Third, it must produce goods and services of satisfactory quality and at a price that will attract and hold the customers whose purchases are the sole source of payroll and profit. Fourth, about half of all the corporation's pre-tax earnings go to the Federal government; for example, to earn one dollar for the stockholder, the enterprise must collect two dollars from the customer above and beyond production costs and pay one of those dollars in Federal taxes. Fifth, it must pay its share of the local taxes needed for the upkeep of the community in which its physical facilities are located.

These responsibilities must be met just to stay in business. No others can be given priority over them. And, when properly viewed, they are of basic social value to the community and to the nation.

But business is heavily criticized for its "selfishness" in not taking a more active part in improving the environment and the conditions of the "underprivileged." The public relations image of business is at an all-time low, and this is one of the reasons.

Naturally, this poor public image is a matter of great concern to management. Every corporation would like to be considered a "good citizen" by everyone. The question is: "Where is the money to come from?" The usual answer from the critics is: "Out of swollen profits."

For this argument to be valid, there must be "swollen profits." Let us look at the record. Here are the latest Department of Commerce figures on the profit per dollar of sales of all United States corporations, except banks, insurance companies, and other financial businesses:

**PROFIT PER $1 OF SALES**

|  | Before Income Taxes | After Income Taxes | . Margin of Profit |
|---|---|---|---|
| 1963 | $.055 | $.029 | 2.9% |
| 1964 | .058 | .032 | 3.2% |
| 1965 | .062 | .036 | 3.6% |
| 1966 | .061 | .036 | 3.6% |
| 1967 | .055 | .032 | 3.2% |
| 1968 | .055 | .029 | 2.9% |
| 1969 | .046 | .023 | 2.3% |
| 1970 | .036 | .018 | 1.8% |
| 1971 | .040 | .021 | 2.1% |
| 1972 | .041 | .022 | 2.2% |
| 1973 | .052 | .027 | 2.7% |

So, we get back to the question: "Where is the money for additional 'social responsibilities' to come from?" Unless there is tax relief or other incentives to the corporations, the only answer is higher prices, and in either of these cases, the public would pay the bill and the corporations would get the credit.

If the public, and a corporation's customers in particular, would be willing to pay higher prices, it would be all right with management. It has not, however, worked that way. Everytime selling prices are raised, a new wave of criticism hurts the public image of the corporation involved, and furthermore, higher prices always involve the risk of losing customers.

All the foregoing leads to the conclusion that, for the national welfare and prosperity, business should be very careful and selective in assuming new "social responsibilities." The prime responsibilities that are now being met in the course of normal operation involve their own important social benefits, which must not be endangered, even by highly desirable ecological and social programs.

While business has a role to play in solving these problems, there should be more public understanding of why management cannot always shoulder additional social responsibilities alone.

# THE BUSINESS INTELLECT
## "VERSUS" THE INTELLECTUAL

Man's material welfare depends upon the production and exchange of goods and services. This, in turn, depends upon peopel who know how to raise capital and to combine men, materials, and machinery into what is called business, meet the payroll, pay the taxes, and operate profitably within the constraints of the law. These men must be intensely practical. Their actions must be governed by cause and effect, and weighed in the light of probable risks and probable rewards. Their judgement must be guided by balanced bookkeeping. These kinds of men are the architects and builders of prosperity.

Man's cultural welfare depends upon the creation of such things as art, music, drama, literature, and upon philosophical conjecture about life. Many of the people who create these art forms and think these thoughts usually have little business sense, and often, very little appreciation for those who do. Many of them find it difficult to understand why the lack of money should be allowed to interfere with cultural and social progress. They seem to be unaware that cultural and social progress can exist only in a society that produces an economic surplus.

Does it not seem irrational for cultural leaders to be opposed to the business leaders whose managerial efforts create the material wealth that helps to nurture and support art and culture?

Since business and art and culture benefit and enrich each other, individuals in each field should make the effort to better understand one another.

This requires better communications between intellectual businessmen and business-like intellectuals.

# WHAT BIG BUSINESS MUST DO
# TO IMPROVE ITS IMAGE

One of the most potent weapons in the hands of anti-private enterprise propagandists is the widely believed charge that big business rakes in "huge," "excessive," "unwarranted," or "swollen" profits. Public opinion polls in recent years consistently have shown that the public believes manufacturing profit per dollar of sales averages 30 per cent or more annually. No wonder so many Americans believe that business could clean up the environment and take on new broad social responsibilities without raising prices, if it only would do so. But United States Department of Commerce figures show that manufacturing "gross" or pre-tax profits in recent years have averaged about 11 per cent, and only a little more than 5 per cent in net or after-tax profit— and of that slender percentage, perhaps half was used to finance new equipment rather than being distributed to stockholders. Of the remaining 89 per cent of total income, 3 out of every 4 dollars went for payroll and the rest to cover non-labor, non-profit costs. Of the total amount divisible between payroll and profit, at least 9 out of every 10 dollars went to payroll. In fact, profit levels have not been sufficient to provide the investment needed to keep the nation's physical plant up to date, let alone take on additional costly responsibilities. Why isn't this generally recognized?

Part of the problem lies in the traditional "earnings report." This report, typically issued on a quarterly and an annual basis, is narrowly focused on those financial aspects of a company's operation that are of interest to present and potential stockholders. It was not designed to put profit and payroll in perspective, and in fact, the traditional earnings report tends to help foster the illusion of big profits. It does this because a good "report card" helps ensure present management's tenure as well as the company's ability to attract investment capital and to obtain loans, so naturally management tries to make earnings look as good as possible.

This is a question of accounting procedures and of emphasis

on strong points rather than deception, but nevertheless, it tends to make earnings look better from this narrow viewpoint than they would from an overall perspective.

The way traditional earnings reports appear in publications also tends to exaggerate the size of overall profits. Only very brief summaries of a tiny percentage of all earnings reports issued appear in most periodicals, and since average performance is scarcely "news," a high proportion of these tend to be strong performance reports. At any given time, a few companies will post outstanding earnings because of favorable market developments, new cost-saving production techniques, or a vastly superior product, and it is easy to assume these standouts one reads about are typical of the business community.

Both economic growth and inflation also need to be taken into account. When report after report says "Record Earnings," who stops to reflect that, in a growing economy, business will post, on balance, both "record" sales and earnings in successive periods—except during recessions. For that matter who considers that workers will achieve, on balance, "record" income levels? Inflation does the same thing to the "business" dollar that it does to the "consumer" dollar—business may have more of them, but they do not buy as much—and what wage-earner is mollified by the fact that wage rates and personal income are at "record levels?"

Traditionally, company earnings are reported as a percentage increase over, or decline from, those of the comparable period a year earlier. If that earlier period was poor, the percentage increase might be sensational, yet the earnings as a percentage of the sales dollar could still be low. "Earnings up 40 per cent" might be both accurate and newsworthy, as well as unusual, but what were earnings a year earlier? How do they compare, as a percentage of the sales dollar, with those of two, five, and ten years ago? For most firms, the answer is they are much lower than a decade ago. Also, that "40 per cent" is all too easy to interpret as a percentage of the sales dollar instead of just the increase over net profits of a year earlier.

Yet despite its shortcomings and the ominous threat to business implied in the finds of the opinion polls, most businesses continue to put out the traditional earnings report. Perhaps these firms hesitate to detail their payroll costs for competitive reasons, perhaps because they are reluctant to expend the time, money, and effort necessary to do so and to develop a format for their earnings report that would be understandable to the average person.

Whatever the reasons, by not providing this kind of factual information, big business has in effect helped forge the potent "swollen profits" weapon used so effectively against it. No group or segment of the society can perform well or prosper when a major part of the population is suspicious of or hostile towards it. No matter that steps to "curb excessive profits" would stultify growth and hurt everyone—businessman, worker, and plain citizen alike—as long as large numbers of people believe that profits are excessive, there will be attempts to trim them. Since no one else is really in a position to do so, it is up to business to set the record straight, to restore its credibility, and to refurbish its public image.

It is too late for business to merely assert the truth—that truth must now be proved with documented information that puts both profit and payroll in proper perspective.

Clearly, big business must do a much better job of conveying its role, its responsibilities, its contributions, and its operating needs, including reasonable profits, to the public than it has in the past.

# GLOSSARY
# OF ECONOMIC
# TERMINOLOGY

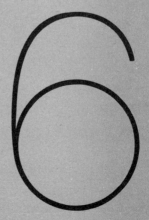

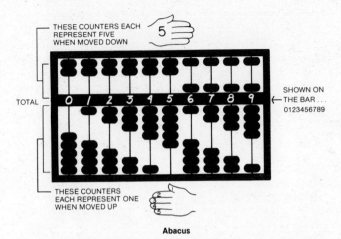

**Abacus**

**Abacus** — An ancient tool to aid mental energy in doing arithmetic. Used in Medieval Europe and still in use in various Oriental countries such as China.

The abacus adapts the age-old principle of using the five fingers of each hand to count from 1 to 10 with sliding beads substituting for fingers.

Each of the sliding beads above the bar counts as 5 when moved down. Each of the sliding beads in the lower section count as 1 when moved up to the bar. In the illustration, as an example, a total of 123456789 is recorded on the bar.

During the early centuries of the Christian era, the Hindus of India formulated the principle of position in relation to a decimal to designate value, each place to the left of the decimal point representing a multiplication by ten, and each place to the right representing a division by ten. In using the abacus the decimal point is placed in any desired location.

**Acceleration Clause** — A written clause in a note, bond, or mortgage that advances the date for total payment because of some possible breach of condition or default by the debtor.

**Accommodation** — A bank loan that is usually made based upon the borrower's line of credit. The borrower's line of credit, or the total amount of funds that he may be loaned, is determined beforehand by the bank.

**Accountants** — People who design, prepare, and interpret books of accounts used by business to record its transactions.

**Accounting** — The art of designing, keeping, and interpreting books of account.

**Accounts**

**Accounts** — A set of books in which is recorded information concerning where certain things came from, where they went to, and the number of dollars involved in the transaction.

**Accounts Payable** — Listed on the balance sheet under "current liabilities" and reflect the unpaid amounts of goods and services purchased by a business from its creditors. Unpaid long-term installment purchases or cash borrowings of any kind are not included under accounts payable.

**Accounts Receivable** — The assets account on the balance sheet that are the amounts currently owed to a firm by its customers for goods or services purchased or rented by the customer for other than cash, for example credit. Accounts receivable do not include amounts due on notes.

**Accrued Interest** — Unpaid interest owed on a bond, promissory notes, and other similar instruments, since the last interest payment was made. The value of the instrument is the market price plus accrued interest.

**Accumulated Interest** — Earned interest installments on such debts as bonds and mortgages that have already come due and are payable but which have not yet been paid.

**Act of God** — An incident resulting from natural causes, without man's intervention, that could not have been prevented by human foresight and precautions. Examples are storms, lightning, and earthquakes.

**Actuary** — A technical, and particularly, mathmetical expert in life insurance and related fields. He is responsible for the calculation of premiums, policy reserves, and other duties, including applying the theory of probability to the business of insurance and advising in cases involving questions of probability.

**Ad Valorem** — A Latin term meaning according to value. A customs duty on an import that is based upon the declared value of the good. An ad valorem duty is a fixed percentage of the foreign or domestic value of the imported good.

**Advertising** — The use of a variety of media and techniques to promote the sale of goods, services or ideas to consumers, businesses, and governments. A major part of advertising takes the form of space bought by the advertiser in the printed media or air time in the electronic media. (See Public Relations.)

**Affiliate** — A company that is closely connected with another company through such means as a controlling stock interest or common management. Holding companies and subsidiaries can be affiliates. (See Subsidiary.)

**Agency Shop** — A factory or other business establishment where non-members of a labor union pay a monthly charge to the union as a condition of employment. The labor union and the management decides what the charge will be through collective bargaining. (See Closed Shop, Union Shop, and antonym, Open Shop.)

**Agent** — An individual or company that is empowered to act for another. For example, a sales agent is authorized by a company to sell its products or services for a commission even though he may not be an employee of the company he represents. (See Broker.)

**Allotment** — The amount or share of securities, either stocks or bonds, that an investment house or syndicate assigns to a subscriber. The subscriber may be an individual or a group of people who are members of a syndicate.

**Amendment** — Generally, a revision or proposed change in something. An addition to, subtraction from, or substitution for a formal motion or resolution at an assembly. Written documents, such as the United States Constitution or corporate by-laws, also can be amended.

**Amortization** — The gradual liquidation of a debt, usually by equal, regular payments over a specific period of time. For example, the payment of a financial obligation on an installment basis. (See Depreciation and Depletion.)

**Anarchism** — A political philosophy that all government is bad, and that people are basically good and would get along better without government laws and restraints. Its followers propose the abolition of government by revolution if necessary.

**Annual Report** — The formal financial statement issued yearly by a corporation to stockholders. It shows assets, liabilities, earnings, and prospects for the coming year.

**Annuity** — The periodic and fixed payment of money to a beneficiary from a fund. Usually, an annuity is established by an individual for himself or his heirs through a money contribution at one time or contributions over a number of years. Provisions for an annuity are often included in a life insurance policy.

**Appraisal** — An estimate of the value of a property either by its owners or by a government authority. (See Assessed Valuation.)

**Appreciation** — An increase in the market value of property or mediums of exchange due to economic or related causes, which may prove to be either temporary or permanent. For example, a house may appreciate due to its location in a particular part of a town.

**Arbitrage** — The practice of simultaneously buying and selling foreign exchange, commodities, or securities in two or more marketplaces to take advantage of price differences. Such differences must be large enough to cover transactions, transportation, taxes, tariffs, and similar costs plus a profit. Risk lies in misjudging costs or in possible price changes during the time lag between issuing buy and sell orders and their execution. Arbitrage tends to quickly equalize prices in all markets after allowance for any associated costs.

**Arbitration** — The process by which management and labor have their differences settled by a third party called an arbitrator. Usually, a Federal official is the arbitrator between the disputants, and the result is an United States collective bargaining contract.

**Arrears** — A debt or other liability that is due but has not been paid; past due debts.

Articles of
Incorporation

**Articles of Incorporation** — A formal document issued to a corporation by the appropriate officers of a state to operate within that state. The Articles are issued after a certificate of incorporation is prepared and filed with the state by the individuals establishing a corporation. Both businesses and organizations such as educational foundations can incorporate. The Articles and the certificate of incorporation are generally known as the corporation's charter. They contain essentially the same information including: the nature of the corporation; its incorporators and location; and, character and amount of capital stock to be authorized and issued by the corporation.

**Artifact** — Any object made by humans, such as works of art, tools, weapons, and utensils. Artifacts help scientists determine the lifestyle and estimate the stage of progress of prehistoric men and earlier civilizations.

**Assessed Valuation** — A monetary valuation of real and personal property by a governmental authority, such as a county or township assessor. The valuation is made to determine the amount of general property tax the owner of the property will pay. Assessing the value of a property is a technique designed to establish a "fair market" value without actually selling the property. This figure or some percentage of it is then used as the basis for levying the tax. (See Appraisal.)

**Assessment** — A monetary demand upon the owners of a property or a business to pay in extra money for some special purpose. For example, government may impose a tax assessment upon property owners to pay for the operating expenses of public schools.

**Assets** — Everything a corporation owns or is owed. Cash, materials and inventories are called current assets; buildings and machinery are fixed assets. From the standpoint of economics, everything owned by a corporation is used as a tool, either of production or exchange. (See antonym, Liabilities.)

Assets

**At the Market** — Instructions to buy or sell a security at the best possible price in the current market.

**Auction Sale** — A sale in which, generally, there is one seller offering his goods to the highest of many bidders. An auction sale is conducted by an auctioneer who permits buyers to make oral bids for the goods being auctioned. Auction sales are advertised in advance and are usually open to the public.

**Auditing** — (Also Audit) A careful professional examination of books of accounts and the records from which the books are kept to see that they are accurate and proper. Audits generally are conducted by accountants or Certified Public Accountants known as Auditors.

**Authorized Stock** — The total number of shares of stock that can be issued by a corporation, according to its certificate of incorporation. The certificate may be amended by the corporation's shareholders to increase the amount of authorized stock. Often, a corporation does not issue all its authorized stock. Some of it may be kept in reserve for future financing.

**Automation** — Applies to the use of mechanical equipment often in combination with high-speed computers to produce goods. Automation increases a nation's payroll and productivity, releases employees from repetitive work, and makes them available for more creative employment.

**Average Annual Dividend Yield** — The total amount of dividends declared on common stock for one year divided by the average price of that stock for the year.

**Balance of Payments** — An itemized record of all financial transactions during a period of time, usually one year, between one nation and the rest of the nations in the world. Included in balance of payments are gold movements, exports, capital transactions and investments, tourist spending and currency shipments. Nations seek to have a surplus rather than a deficit in their balance of payments.

**Balance of Trade** — The net difference between the value of goods that a nation exports and that which it imports. When a nation's value of exports exceeds its value of imports, the nation is said to have a surplus or "favorable" balance of trade. When the value of imports exceeds the value of exports, the nation is said to have a deficit or "unfavorable" balance of trade.

Does not include foreign investment, government grants and other forms of assistance. These added to Balance of Trade equal Balance of Payments.

```
                          CENTRAL COMPANY
                           BALANCE SHEET
                         DECEMBER 31, 19X5

CURRENT ASSETS                         CURRENT LIABILITIES
CASH                       $ 15,000    ACCOUNTS PAYABLE              $ 50,000
ACCOUNTS RECEIVABLE          15,000    INCOME TAXES                    20,000
INVENTORIES                  20,000    OTHER ACCRUED LIABILITIES       20,000
PREPAID EXPENSES             15,000    TOTAL CURRENT LIABILITIES       90,000
TOTAL CURRENT ASSETS         65,000
                                       STOCKHOLDERS' EQUITY:
EQUIPMENT                    55,000    COMMON STOCK, $2 PAR VALUE-
LESS ACCUMULATED DEPRECIATION 10,000   20,000 SHARES AUTHORIZED,
                                       10,000 SHARES ISSUED             20,000
NET EQUIPMENT                45,000
                                       TOTAL STOCKHOLDERS' EQUITY       20,000
TOTAL ASSETS               $110,000
                                       TOTAL LIABILITIES AND
                                       EQUITY                         $110,000
```

**Balance Sheet**

**Balance Sheet** — A condensed statement showing in dollars the nature and amount of a company's assets, liabilities and capital, and the ownership interest of its stockholders. It shows what the company owns, what it owes to others, and what it is owed by others.

**Balanced Budget** — A budget in which during a given period of time, expenditures are equal to revenues. In government, a balanced budget is an annual budget that allows government spending to be no higher than the amount of revenues a government has on hand and collects in taxes. When government spending is greater than government revenues, there is deficit spending. If the deficit is covered by "earned money," it does not represent an addition to the money supply and is, therefore, not inflationary. If the deficit is covered by newly created money, it is an addition to the money supply, and, therefore, it is inflationary, reducing the value of all "earned money."

**Bank Acceptance** — A draft or bill of exchange accepted by a bank, person, company, or corporation. On the face of the document is the signature of the debtor against whom the draft or bill is drawn, indicating his intention to pay.

**Bank Account** — The funds that an individual, company, or other organization deposits in a bank. Examples include: checking (demand deposits) and savings (time deposit) accounts.

**Bank Draft** — An amount of money drawn by one bank upon another bank. A bank draft is a sight or demand draft that is payable immediately upon presentation. Bank drafts are often used in commercial transactions and usually have a time limit on their negotiability.

**Bankruptcy** — The state or condition of a business or an individual of being insolvent or unable to meet financial debts. Either the debtor or his creditors can initiate bankruptcy proceedings by filing a petition of bankruptcy under the National Bankruptcy Act. A Federal Court declares bankruptcy and turns the assets of a debtor over to a receiver or trustee for the administration and the orderly payment of debts to creditors or to reorganize the debtor's financial affairs so that he may continue his business. (See Insolvency and antonym, Solvency.)

**Barter** — The direct exchange or trading of one commodity for another without the use of money or reference to price. Barter is an ancient form of exchange. An example of barter is trading one bushel of grain for three chickens.

**Bear Market** — An expression used to describe the stock market when it is experiencing a prolonged, downward trend in stock prices. A speculator who believes stock prices will decline is called a Bear. (See antonym, Bull Market.)

**Bearer Bond** — A bond that does not have the owner's name registered on the books of the company or on the bond. It is payable to the holder.

**Beneficiary** — Generally, an individual or organization who receives the proceeds from a trust or life insurance policy.

**Bid and Asked** — The "bid" is the highest price offered for a security at a given time. The "asked" is the lowest price anyone will take for a security at the same time the "bid" is offered.

A bid is also an offer to buy a good or to perform a service at a specific price. At an auction, people bid on the goods being auctioned. A carpenter may make a bid to do some work on a house.

**Big Board** — A popular term for the New York Stock Exchange.

**Bill of Exchange** — A written negotiable instrument drawn up and signed by the first party (usually a seller of goods or services) and signed by a second party (usually a buyer). The second party agrees to pay whoever legally holds the instrument a specified sum on a specified date.

**BILL of LADING**
From XYZ CO.
DATE ___ NAME OF CARRIER · ABC
CITY CHICAGO, ILL
NUMBER PACKAGES / KIND OF PACKAGE LARGE BOX

**Bill of Lading**

**Bill of Lading** — A receipt issued by a carrier, showing that it has received the goods that are to be transported to a specified destination or person; a contract of transportation between a shipper and a transportation company.

**Bimetallism** — A monetary system in which two metals are freely and concurrently coined and accepted in unlimited quantities for coinage with each kind of coin being made full legal tender, and the ratio value of one metal to the other being set by law. The coined metals are usually gold and silver.

**Black Market** — A market operating in violation of government price and rationing laws.

**Blue Chip** — Common stock in a company nationally known for its ability to make money and pay dividends in good times and bad. (See Gilt-Edged.)

**Blue Sky Laws** — A group of laws enacted to protect the public against frauds.

**Board of Directors** — The persons elected by the stockholders or the owners of a business charged under the company's by-laws with the responsibility of supervising the affairs and operations of the company and establishing its general policies. A director of a company may also be an owner. (See Director.)

**Board of Directors**

**Board Room** — A room for brokers' customers where current prices of leading stocks are posted throughout the day.

**Boiler Room Operation** — High pressure selling of dubious stocks over the telephone.

**Bolshevism** — "Bolshevik" is derived from the Russian word for majority. The Bolsheviks were the extreme left of the pre-revolutionary Russian Social Democratic Party, the other major faction being the Mensheviks. Both groups believed the tools of production should be owned by the workers, but the Bolsheviks insisted on a centralized party—a firmly coherent party of like-minded individuals with tasks they would carry out like soldiers—while the Mensheviks would accept general adherence to party goals and stressed universal suffrage and a democratic constituent assembly—i.e., a representative form of government. The Bolsheviks eventually won out, suppressing the Mensheviks along with all other factions and establishing a government tightly controlled by a small group of the party elite and organizing it so that (1) management of the tools of production was (theoretically) in the hands of the workers, and (2) candidates for the local Soviets or councils were drawn from occupational groups rather than, as elsewhere, from the citizenry at large. At the federal level, the Congress of Soviets was to be much like the federations of constituent republics elsewhere, but the center retained control not only of the usual defense and similar national functions, but also of all economic ones. The term, "Bolshevik," is also sometimes loosely used to denote individuals espousing anarchistic, communistic, or other radical views.

**Bond** — Basically a governmental or corporate I.O.U. or promissory note usually issued in multiples of $1,000. The issuing company, government, or government agent promises to pay the bondholders a specified amount of interest for a specified length of time, and to repay the loan on or before a maturity date. A bondholder is a creditor, not an owner of a company. Thus, bonds usually carry with them a legal right for the people who loaned the money to seize certain assets of the business or force it into bankruptcy if the business fails to repay the loan and the interest. Also, an agreement in which one party guarantees to protect others against loss, as in bail bond, bonding of bank messenger and cashiers, or the bond posted by the administrator of an estate to protect beneficiaries against loss due to malfeasance on his part.

**Bond**

**Book Value** — An accounting term representing an estimate of a company's net worth at some given point in time. The figure is determined by adding all assets (generally excluding such intangibles as good will) then deducting all debts and other liabilities.

**Book Value**

**Book Value Per Share** — The book value of a company divided by the number of common shares outstanding at the company's year end.

**Bottlenecks** — Any condition that, by itself, interrupts or interferes with the production process. Bottlenecks normally take the form of shortages of factors of production that tend to exert influence all out of proportion to their otherwise relative contribution to production. Bottlenecks can occur in materials, in certain management or labor skills, or in tools, and have the result of strongly increasing costs for these factors while disrupting production processes in which they are involved as firms bid for the existing stock of such factors. Since any of these bottlenecks can be relieved by substitutions of new processes, new machinery, or development of new sources for materials in short supply or of alternate materials, adequate depreciation allowances and depreciation schedules are key elements in any approach designed to combat bottlenecks and promote productivity.

Bottlenecks are also a major factor in holding down progress towards industrialization in "underdeveloped" nations where substantial investments in largely non-productive facilities such as roads, seaport facilities, education, railroads, and communications facilities may be necessary to promote productive activities such as manufacturing, mining of ore and raw materials, and economical transfer of agricultural products.

**Boycott** — An organized protest by a group that, by refusing to do business or have other relationships with a person, business, or other group, aims to force concessions or changes in policy or to punish the target of the boycott for past alleged offenses. The term is derived from the name of an Irish land agent, Captain Boycott, who was so treated.

**Break-Even Point** — (Business) The amount of sales, and consequently of production and distribution that, at the prices set, must be reached before a profit is possible.

**Broker** — An independent agent who brings others together to negotiate bargains, agreements or contracts. He himself normally does not own the goods that are to be the subject of negotiations, but receives a commission for his service. Examples include a real estate broker who brings together the buyer and the seller of a house and securities or commodity brokers, who are agents licensed to handle the public's orders to buy and sell securities or commodities. (See Agent.)

**Budget** — A formal, itemized estimate of future incomes and expenses for a definite period of time. Budgets help business, government, and individuals to control expenses and to co-ordinate financial plans and supporting actions and decisions in advance.

**Bull Market** — A term used to describe a stock market where the trend of stock prices is upward. In a Bull Market, optimism among buyers and brokers in the continued increase of stock prices prevails. A speculator who believes stock prices are rising is called a Bull. (See Bear Market.)

**Bullion** — Refined gold and silver in the form of bars or ingots but not minted coins. Most government gold reserves and official international transactions in gold between governments are in gold bullion.

**Bullion**

**Bullionists** — Term applied to the majority of merchants, rulers, and thinkers of the fifteenth and sixteenth centuries who held that the accumulation of money or the metals out of which it was chiefly made—gold or silver bullion—must be the chief objective of national policy. This was a basic tenant of so-called "Mercantilism," which largely held sway in international circles until Adam Smith refuted the argument in his *Wealth of Nations,* published in 1775, pointing out that the real wealth of any nation lay in its "annual labor" and available resources and the skill with which they are employed—that is, in its productivity.

**Business Cycles** — The periodic alternate expansion and contraction in the level of business activity. Business cycles can be characterized by an increase or expansion of business activity to a peak or time of prosperity, and then, the gradual decline or contraction of activity to a low period or time of recession or depression. The low period is then followed by the next cycle, an upturn or expansion and again the downturn or contraction.

**By-Laws** — A set of rules adopted by the stockholders of a company or other organization setting forth the general regulations by which the company or group will function and govern itself. A company's or other incorporated group's by-laws cannot conflict with its Articles of Incorporation.

**Call Loan** — A loan that may be terminated or "called" at any time by the lender or borrower.

**Call to Order** — The formal opening of a meeting of an organization operating under Robert's Rules of Order. Examples include a shareholders' or board of directors' meeting presided over by the chairman of the board or by another appropriate company officer. The chairman rises and states, "the meeting will please come to order."

**Capacity** — The maximum output that a company, an industry, or an economy can reach, given its current level of available human energy and natural resources and available tools. Capacity can be increased by addition of human energy and natural resources and by investment in new, and improved tools, with new and improved tools permitting the fastest and most dramatic increases in capacity. (See Load Factor and Productivity.)

**Capital** — This is an ancient word derived from "capita," meaning number of heads of livestock that a person owned. This was in a period of history when the principal form of productive wealth was livestock. It had no relation to money until things began to be measured and recorded in units of money, early in the seventeenth century. The word "capital" was then applied to all forms of productive wealth, and today it is a synonym for tools of production and exchange. Capital represents all of the things used by workers in the production and exchange of goods and services.

The term also is sometimes loosely used to mean the total assets of an enterprise, in which case it is useful to further subdivide those assets into money capital and property capital.

**Capital Expenditures** — Expenditures of cash or the creation of a liability, such as buying on credit, in exchange for permanent property or another fixed asset in the business. Capital expenditures are investments in land, buildings, machinery, and other equipment.

**Capital Flight** — The movement of commodities—usually gold—from one country to another or the exchange of holdings in one currency for holdings in another for reasons other than investment or commerce (fear of expropriation, devaluation, war, or similar development). It reflects a loss of confidence in a nation's monetary or political stability. Such flights, if large enough, can sometimes help bring about the event feared by disrupting the nation's economic activities. Individuals involved profit only if the outcome they fear occurs, since there are costs involved both in moving gold or exchanging currencies—and if the flight is widespread, the exchange rate may be depressed. During the 1930's, America attracted large quantities of gold from a Europe fearful of Hitler's announced intentions.

**Capital Gain or Capital Loss** — Profit or loss from the sale of a capital asset or securities. A capital gain is taxable income. A capital loss is deductible.

**Capital Stock** — The total amount of stock issued by a corporation to its stockholders. It includes common stock, convertible stock, preferred stock, and participating preferred stock.

**Capital Surplus** — Paid-in surplus, particularly, surplus other than earned surplus. Capital surplus is derived from such sources as sale of capital stock at premium, profit on dealings in a corporation's own stock, donated stock, and appraisal revaluations.

**Capitalism** — Broadly, any system of production and exchange in which tools play an important role. A system in which the workers own the tools they use is personal capitalism, with an example being economies based on so-called "cottage industry." A system in which tools are owned by private individuals but used by others is private capitalism ("capitalism" is often used interchangeably with "private capitalism" to designate a system based on private ownership of all kinds of property and the right of the individual to contract with others and to pursue activities of his own choice for his own profit and well-being. Also called private enterprise.) A system in which tools are owned by the state is called state capitalism. This ownership can be incomplete, as in economies where some but not all industries are nationalized or regulated by the state—also called state socialism—or complete, as under communism.

**Capitalization** — Converting the value of realty or future incomes into current equivalent capital value. The amount determined refers to the capital structure of a corporation.

**Carrying Charge** — The fee charged by a broker for carrying a customer's securities on margin.

**Cartel** — An arrangement based upon an agreement between independent industrial enterprises producing similar goods to form an association, usually on an international level, to control the price, supply, and marketing of a particular product or group of products. Combination is sometimes used as a synonym for cartel, but while cartels are virtually always held to be in violation of United States anti-trust laws, combinations include activities that do not violate these statutes, such as joint or common ventures requiring large amounts of capital undertaken by two or more firms.

**Cash** — Derived from "casse," an Old French word meaning box or chest that came to be used for chests made to hold coins. Strictly defined, cash refers only to "ready money," that is coins or paper money issued by the nation's monetary authorities. These are "legal tender" for all debts and obligations, circulate freely, constitute immediate purchasing power, and, in effect, are "bearer's bonds" in that anyone who holds them can spend them. Currency is often used interchangeably with cash, but currency includes checks, money orders, and similar instruments, many of which can only be transferred by specified individuals. That transferring these instruments is called "cashing" them shows they are not "cash." Money is also often used interchangeably with both cash and currency, although money designates anything generally accepted in exchange for other things and thus is a much broader term. To a business firm's accountant, cash includes coins and paper money, negotiable money orders, checks, and balances on deposit with banks after deducting outstanding checks.

**Cash Assets** — Assets, such as cash on hand and short-term securities, that can be readily converted into cash.

**Cash Flow Per Share** — A company's net income plus non-cash charges against income, such as depreciation and amortization, less any preferred dividends divided by the common stock outstanding at the company's year end.

**Cash Sale** — A Stock Exchange transaction that calls for delivery of the securities the same day. In "regular way" trades, the seller is allowed four business days to make delivery.

**Certificates of Deposit** — Receipts issued by commercial banks for a cash deposit not subject to withdrawal for a stipulated length of time, normally 3 months, 6 months, or one year. Because the bank is assured of the use of the funds for the full stipulated period, CD's normally pay higher interest rates than passbook saving accounts. The CD's of high denomination — $100,000 or more — usually issued by large banks are not subject to interest regulation and can pay what the market demands, and since there is an active secondary market for them, can readily be sold if necessary. Small denomination CD's are subject to interest regulation and normally are not negotiable.

**Charter** — The granting of rights and privileges by a government, usually that of a state, to a business or other organization to incorporate and to transact business or other activity. It also is used to designate a written statement of basic laws or principles and to describe the renting or leasing of a bus, ship, aircraft, or similar vehicle.

**Cheap Money** — Denotes money loaned at relatively low interest rates. Also an expression describing a condition where a relatively high quantity of money is needed to purchase relatively small amounts of goods and services, that is, money is "cheap" — its value low — relative to goods and services. In effect the general price level of goods and services increases while the value of money decreases. (See Easy Money.)

**Closed Shop** — A factory or business in which all prospective employees except management candidates must join the labor union as a condition of employment. Under the Taft-Hartley Act of 1947, closed shops were made illegal for firms engaged in interstate commerce, but the law is not always adhered to. (See Agency Shop, Union Shop, and antonym, Open Shop.)

**Coin** — A piece of metal stamped and marked by the government for use as money. Coins can be full-bodied "specie" — that is, contain gold or silver in amounts equivalent to face value — or they can be "token" — that is, they derive

Coin

much or all of their value from the credibility of the government issuing them rather than having intrinsic value. In the United States, it is illegal to melt down coins and sell the resulting metal.

**Collateral** — An individual's or business' real or personal property pledged as part or full guarantee of payment for an obligation or loan. If an individual or business defaults on his obligation or loan, his creditor is allowed to take what the borrower pledged as collateral as full or partial payment.

**Collateral Trust Bond** — A Bond secured by collateral deposited with a trustee.

**Collective Bargaining** — The process of negotiations between employers and employees' representatives, such as labor union officials, through which a written agreement is made on conditions of employment, including wages, working conditions, hours of work, retirement benefits, and vacation time. Collective bargaining agreements are made either on an individual company or industry-wide basis.

**Collectivism** — A social and political system that places much or all of a nation's economic power in the hands of a central authority, usually the government. Such power may be exercised through outright ownership by the state as in the case of communism and some forms of socialism, or it can take the form of economic planning or control so extensive that freedom of contract is absent, even though private property is maintained in part or full, as under Fascism and some forms of socialism.

**Commerce** — The buying and selling of goods and services and anything related to the production, exchange, and financial transactions involving the goods and services. Commerce is usually characterized as buying and selling on a national or international scale; often referred to simply as trade.

**Commercial Paper** — Refers to notes of various denominations issued by corporations to or through note brokers or commercial paper houses and purchased by banks and other investors in all parts of the country. Normally these involve blocks of hundreds of thousands of dollars.

**Commission** — Compensation paid by a business or individual to an agent or broker for a service rendered. The commission is usually a percentage of the amount of money involved in the transaction. For example, stockbrokers receive commissions when they buy or sell a share of stock for a customer.

**Commodities**

**Commodities** — Any physical goods that are commonly bought and sold. This includes cultivated crops and animal products, manufactured products, and processed materials but not land, buildings, or undeveloped natural resources.

**Commodity Exchange** — An organization of traders who buy and sell contracts for the immediate or future delivery of such products as grains, cotton, hogs, sugar, and coffee. These contracts are bought and sold through and guaranteed by an official clearinghouse, such as the Chicago Board of Trade or Chicago Mercantile Exchange. No products are delivered to the clearinghouse.

**Common Shares Outstanding** — The total number of shares outstanding, excluding shares held in the company's treasury, at the company's calendar, or fiscal year end.

**Common Stock**

**Common Stock** — Securities representing ownership interest in a corporation. Unless otherwise specified, owners of common stock are entitled to vote in the management of a corporation. If the corporation has also issued preferred stock, both common and preferred have ownership rights, but the preferred normally has prior claim on dividends and, in the event of liquidation, assets.

**Communism** — A political and economic system under which each person's share of the production is measured by his needs, rather than by the amount he produces. Initially, a central government owns the tools of production and decides what each person produces and needs. Eventually, central government is supposed to wither away. The historical examples of true communism are few, and these few did not long survive. Modern communism is a form of state capitalism based on absolute and forced obedience to government in all matters.

**Communist Manifesto** — A document written by Karl Marx and Friedrich Engels in 1848 at the behest of a secret international organization that called itself the League of the Just. Most of the benefits promised labor as a consequence of seizure of power have long since been realized in capitalist nations, including the 8-hour day, social insurance, higher pay, improved working conditions, and greater job security.

**Company** — A group of people organized to carry on some business activity. Corporations and partnerships are companies.

**Competition** — (Economics) A spontaneous method of controlling private interest for the public benefit that consists of unfettered rivalry for income. That rivalry must be open to all, and takes as many forms as there are opportunities to seek income. Competition imposes a basic constraint on all active participants—they must give or seem to give more than their rivals in proportion to what is asked in return. This requires operating efficiently; that is, at low cost consistent with necessary features and quality. Although competition may waste resources in the short run, it conserves them in the long run, increasing both individual and national income by forcing others, and ultimately, the economy, to operate more efficiently. (See antonyms, Monopoly, and Monopsony.)

**Conglomerate** — A large corporation that has grown by purchasing and mergering with other companies and corporations. The product lines of a conglomerate are generally diversified, allowing the conglomerate to be active in a variety of different business enterprises, thus protecting itself against the dangers of product specialization and making possible, although not assuring, the advantages of superior management and economies of scale.

**Conservative** — From the Latin words *com*, "with" plus *servare*, "to guard." Broadly defined, means to keep from being damaged, lost or wasted, tending to conserve, moderate, prudent. In political-economic terms a person who strongly supports private property rights and individual freedom, who supports change, but gradual change based upon the lessons of experience, and who wishes to limit the role of government to a few indispensable spheres in the political, economic, and social lives of the nation's people. (See Reactionary.)

**Consignment** — A shipment of goods from the consignor to the consignee on condition that the latter will pay the former when the goods are sold.

**Consumer** — The person who actually makes use of goods and services. The consumer is distinguished from the customer in that the customer is the person who makes or authorizes the purchase, and may or may not be the ultimate consumer.

**Consumer Price Index** — The monthly index of prices, compiled and maintained by the United States Bureau of Labor Statistics, showing changes in prices paid by urban families and individuals for some 300 goods and services. It is expressed as a percentage of the average price for those same goods and services that urban consumers paid in a given base year. It gives a partial indication of the cost of living for urban consumers.

**Consumption** — The use of material goods or services, often natural resources, as an end in itself, rather than for the production of another good or service. For example, the use of water for drinking as opposed to running an electric generator would be consumption.

**Contingent Liability** — An obligation that may be imposed upon an individual, corporation, or partnership because of some past event or accident that may occur again in the future.

Contract

**Contract** — An oral or written agreement between two or more persons or parties enforceable under law to do or not to do something. To be valid and binding, a contract must be entered into by competent parties, be bound by a consideration, possess mutuality of agreement, and cover a legal and moral act. For example, in a business sales contract, a supplier agrees to provide a purchaser a product or a service in accordance with their agreement.

**Contract Bond** — A bond that guarantees the faithful performance of a construction contract and the payment of all labor and material bills related to the performance. In situations where two bonds are required, the one to cover performance is known as the performance bond, and the other to cover payment of labor and material is known as the payment bond.

**Contractual Liability Insurance** — Insurance that protects an individual or business against claims that may arise as the result of contractual liability. For example, a manufacturer of nuts and bolts may have a signed contract with a purchaser against claims that may arise out of the use of these nuts and bolts in the manufacture of the purchaser's product.

**Contracyclical Policies** — Steps taken by the government to try to counter major swings in the business cycle, and include such actions as tightening credit and reducing government spending in inflationary periods and expanding them in downturns. (See Pump Priming, Fiscal Policy, Monetary Policy.)

**Convertible** — A bond, debenture or preferred share that may be exchanged by the owner for common stock or another security in accordance with the terms of the issue.

**Convertible Money** — Currency that may be redeemed for gold or silver at a stated exchange rate from the government that issued the currency.

**Copyright** — An exclusive right granted by law to control the printing and the selling of a literary manuscript or artistic work for a period of 28 years. At the end of that time, the copyright may be renewed for another 28 years.

**Corporation** — A legal body entitled to do business as if it were an individual. Requirements for forming a corporation vary from state to state, but usually three or more officers, a president, a vice-president, and a secretary/treasurer are named in the articles of incorporation. Ownership by individual persons in a corporation is determined by the percentage to the value of the total shares issued. The introduction of the idea of using a corporation made it possible for large investments to be made when the costs of the needed tools exceeded what one or a few persons could afford. Thus, large ventures could be launched with many people participating in projected profits while at the same time spreading the risk amongst many in case of losses.

**Costs** — The costs of any business are five in number:
1. Cost of goods and services bought from others necessary for the production and exchange of the company's goods and services. This cost includes rent and interest on borrowed money.
2. The cost of human energy used up in the production and exchange of the company's goods and services. This cost is called such things as payroll, bonuses, and benefits.
3. The cost of the tools wearing out or being used up. This is called such things as obsolescence, depreciation, and amortization.
4. Cost of the payments collected from the customer on behalf of government. These are called taxes and fees.
5. Cost of payments collected from the customer on behalf of the owners of the tools as reward for the use of the tools. This is variously called profit, dividends, return on investment, and returns to equity.

All costs of an established business must be collected from the customer, and if the customer is unable or unwilling to pay them, the business must fail.

**Coupon Bonds** — Bonds with interest coupons attached. The coupons are clipped as they come due and are presented for payment of interest.

**Craft or Trade Union** — A labor union that generally restricts its membership to persons engaged in a particular craft or skill, such as carpentry, electricial work, or plumbing. (See Industrial Union.)

**Credit** — (Business) From the word "credo," to believe. Credit involves giving someone something without receiving immediate payment, trusting the receiver to make payment at a later date.

(Line of) A practice of commercial banks to permit business to write checks against the bank up to a certain amount, with the expectation that the money will be repaid. Also extended to individuals by many banks.

(Bookkeeping) An entry in the book of accounts showing that something has been disposed of and recording the amount involved. (See antonyms, Debit and Debt.)

**Creditor** — An individual or business to whom a debt is owed.

**Cumulative Preferred** — A stock providing that if one or more dividends are omitted, the omitted dividends must be paid before dividends are resumed on common stock.

Currency

**Currency** — The term is sometimes used to designate only *cash*—coins and paper money issued by the government. But in both current usage and as implied by the meaning of the Latin word it is derived from (currere, "to run") currency designates all instruments of general acceptance that "run" in circulation, including checks, money orders, and similar negotiable instruments. In modern economies, most business transactions are carried out by means of checks and other non-cash currency.

**Current Assets** — Assets such as cash, accounts receivable and merchandise inventory that may be converted into cash or other assets within a relatively short period of time, usually one year or less.

**Current Liabilities** — Short-term debts and other obligations that are to be paid out of current assets or transferred to income within a short period of time, usually one year or less.

**Current Position** — An itemized listing of a firm's current assets and current liabilities.

**Customer** — A person who exchanges something of value he has for the goods and services offered for sale by another. The customer purchase is the final act of production and exchange for any given company. The customer may be another company that will either process the product further or offer it for re-sale, so there may be several additional transactions before the product reaches the customer who uses or "consumes" it, that is, the consumer. The activity and prosperity of any business depends upon the willingness and ability of its direct customers to make the purchases, with companies at each station in the production and exchange process being ultimately dependent upon purchases by the consumer. Ever since man stopped producing only for himself and had to find other men who would buy what he produced, the customer has been the source of employment. The management of business decides *who* is on the payroll, but its customers decide *how many* and *how much* they may receive.

**Debasement** — A government reduction in the amount of gold or silver contained in a nation's coins used for legal tender.

**Debenture** — Debenture literally means "they are due." A debenture is a security or written record of debt. They are commonly loans to a company issued without security. Debentures have a fixed rate of interest and a principal repayable after a number of years.

**Debit** — An entry in the book of accounts showing that something has been acquired by the business and must be accounted for when it is disposed of. (See Credit.)

**Debt** — A liability or obligation to pay or return something. The condition of owing something. Acceptance of one of the two conditions involved in a credit transaction: to obtain credit is to incur debt and to grant credit means the other party to the transaction incurs debt. Most financial assets held or sought by individuals or firms are or will become the debt of others. (See antonym, Credit.)

**Debt Ratio** — A measure showing the relation between long-term debt and total capital, which is expressed as a percentage. The percentage is arrived at by dividing long-term debt by total capital.

Deed

**Deed** — A legal document used to transfer the title to real property from a seller to a buyer.

**Deficit** — A word to denote that a business or government has paid out more dollars than it has received in a given time period. The difference between the totals of all payments and of all receipts is the amount of the deficit. (See antonym, Surplus.)

**Deficit Spending** — Spending more money than received in revenues. When a government engages in deficit spending, it can obtain the necessary funds in one of two basic ways. First, it can borrow from individuals or institutions (other than banks), thereby, shifting purchasing power from the private to the public sector. Spending is financed from the existing money supply, and thus is not inflationary. Second, the government finances the spending by giving notes to commercial banks and receiving checking accounts in the amount of the notes. This creates new money and is inflationary.

**Deflation** — A condition under which the volume of currency or credit is reduced. Whether or not this decrease results in lower selling prices depends upon the volume of goods and services for sale and the intensity of the desire of the people to exchange their money or credit for goods and services. (See antonym, Inflation.)

**Demand Deposits** — Bank deposits that can be withdrawn by the depositor at any time. A checking account is an example of a demand deposit.

**Democracy — Compared with Republic** — When these words first came into use as labels for contrasting forms of government, supporters of the democratic form believed that no man's judgment and ability in governmental affairs was any better than that of any other man. Any citizen was considered to be as good an administrator as any other. The republicans, on the other hand, believed that better government could be secured if the decisions were made by men whose greater education, experience, etc., supposedly resulted in their exercising better judgement. In a democracy, decisions were to be made by all the people, at mass meetings, town meetings, etc., while in a republic decisions were to be made by popularly elected representatives, selected for their supposedly special abilities. These men had to be re-elected at regular intervals, and if people were not pleased with their performance, they could be rejected at the polls. In ancient days neither system allowed all the people to vote; women, slaves, people with no property, "foreigners", etc., were excluded. In modern usage, however, "democracy" and "republic" have lost their historical meanings. They are now used interchangeably as meaning almost the same thing. They, therefore, have no precise meaning. There are two differences of opinion between the supporters of the democracy idea and the supporters of the republic idea. The first is the amount of power that should be exercised by the Federal Government. Believers in "democracy" recommend the very powerful Federal Government, while believers in "republicanism" support the idea that most of the power should be exercised by the elected officials of the towns and states. The second difference is a sociological one and revolves around the question of whether people of exceptional ability should be allowed to earn and keep exceptionally large incomes. The "democracy" group supports the practice of taxing away the greater part of large incomes. Supporters of the "republic" viewpoint believe that this practice is a form of robbery and is not good for the nation's economic health. It is important to note that in the United States today people supporting the "democracy" and "republic" viewpoints are not necessarily members of the Democratic or Republican Party. There are democrats in the Republican Party and republicans in the Democratic Party.

**Depletion** — A word meaning the using up of a natural resource used in production, such as gold or iron ore, coal, oil, and other minerals. Depletion is recorded in the books of accounts in dollars, and the same amount of dollars is usually taken from income and set aside in a fund presumably to be used for finding replacements for the depleted resources. Depletion allowances are non-taxable income. (See Amortization.)

**Depreciation** — The loss in value and usefulness of tools as they grow old and wear out; theoretically, the difference between the replacement cost of something new and its present value. Deductions from taxable earnings to compensate a company for the loss in value of assets due to wearing out, growing old, etc. (See Amortization.)

**Depreciation Rate** — A company's total amount of depreciation, depletion, and amortization charged to its income during the year, which is expressed as a percentage of the company's gross plant, including: buildings, equipment, and land, at year end.

**Depression** — A protracted period of low business activity characterized by widespread unemployment, low production, a contraction of credit, a sharp curtailment in consumer buying, government intervention, and business and consumer pessimism. As exemplified by the depression of 1929-1933, depressions can last for years and can have worldwide repercussions.

**Devaluation** — The action by which a government reduces the "gold content" of its monetary unit; that is, the value of its monetary unit relative to the value of standard units of gold (i.e., gold costs more in terms of that nation's monetary unit). Since it has the immediate effect of reducing the value of the nation's currency in relation to the currencies of other nations, this is normally done in an effort to stem imports and encourage exports by making the nation's goods less expensive to foreigners and foreign goods more expensive to its citizens. Devaluation can only be successful if the nation's trading partners do not devalue their currencies by a similar amount, which would restore the original exchange rates, but leave the value or price of gold higher in terms of each currency that is devalued. Since 1973, exchange rates have been permitted to "float" within certain limits, thus adjusting to supply and demand and permitting overvalued currencies to devalue gradually. (See antonym, Revaluation.)

**Director** — Person elected by shareholders at the annual meeting to direct company policies. The directors elect the chairman, appoint the president, vice presidents, and all other operating officers. (See Board of Directors.)

**Discretionary Account** — An account in which the customer gives the broker or someone else discretion as to the purchase and sale of his securities.

**Discretionary Order** — The customer specifies what is to be bought or sold. His agent is free to act as to time and price.

**Disintermediation** — The process under which investors withdraw deposits earning relatively low interest to put them into higher-yielding investments. Since it works to reduce the total of funds savings institutions have on hand to finance mortgages and home improvements during times of high interest rates and "tight money," disintermediation tends to reduce housing starts and construction activity during such periods along with higher construction costs traceable, in part, to the higher cost of money. It also works to hold down transfers of existing homes and buildings.

**Distribution** — (Commerce) The diffusion of goods through normal trade channels.
(Economics) The apportionment of the total income of a society among the factors of production, including wages, rent, interest, and profit, or among individuals.
(Securities) The selling of a large block of stock over a period of time without unduly depressing the market price of the stock.

**Diversification** — The participation of a single business in the production and marketing of two or more different kinds of goods and services. It is done to help avoid the risk of sharp fluctuations in revenue that might occur due to changes in overall business or single market activities.
In securities, the investment in a variety of securities representing different companies and industries to avoid being tied to the business fortunes of one company or one industry.

**Dividend** — The payment designated by the Board of Directors to be distributed pro rata among the shares outstanding. On preferred shares, it is generally a fixed amount. On common shares, the dividend varies with the fortunes of the company. Dividends are paid out of the earnings or profits of a company.

**Dividends Declared Per Share** — The common stock dividends per share declared but not necessarily paid, during a company's fiscal year.

**Dow Theory** — A theory that attempts to forecast securities market price trends based upon past market price performance as a guide to investors. Critics have pointed out that it makes little sense to use stock price changes to forecast stock price changes, and have sought other indicators, with growth or contraction of the money supply being one such approach. Historically, both changes in the money supply and stock price trends have consistently preceeded business cycle changes, the former somewhat ahead of the latter.

**CENTRAL BANK**

SOLE BILL OF EXCHANGE

$ 1,000.00   DATE June 1, 1980   NO. 10

10 DAYS AFTER July 1, 1980 of this SOLE BILL OF EXCHANGE
pay to the order of CENTRAL BANK
ABC Corp.
VALUE RECEIVED AND CHARGE THE SAME TO ACCOUNT OF
TO Don Jones

AUTHORIZED SIGNATURE

Draft

**Draft** — A written order for a specific sum of money by the drawer or creditors, ordering the drawee or debtor to pay the money to a payee. Often the drawer and the payee are the same person. Drafts are customarily forwarded to a bank, which presents it to the drawee for payment. A sight draft is payable at once. Time drafts are payable on a fixed date. An arrival draft is paid by the drawee upon receiving the goods.

**Earnings** — The amount collected from the customer on behalf of the owners of the tools. Also called pure profit.
In accounting, a broad term denoting an increase in wealth resulting from the operation of an enterprise.

**Earnings Per Share as Reported** — The per share earnings reported by a company at fiscal year end adjusted for all stock splits and dividends.

**Earnings Per Share Year-End** — A figure that is arrived

at by dividing a company's net income, less any preferred dividends paid or accumulated, by the number of common shares outstanding at year end.

**Earnings Report** — A statement—also called an income statement—issued by a company showing its earnings or losses over a given period.

**Easy Money** — Money obtained from a bank at a relatively low interest rate due to high reserves among banks. (See Cheap Money.)

**Economic Indicator** — An index based upon surveys or reports of levels of various kinds of business activities that is used to forecast business conditions by monitoring changes or trends in that index. The three major types of indicators are: *leading* indicators such as new orders; *co-incident* indicators such as the rate of unemployment; and, *lagging* indicators such as capital expenditures. Since they are based upon past performances, they merely indicate the present level of business and must be used with care in projecting future business conditions.

A diffusion index is a single index number derived from a group of index numbers—all either lagging, co-incident, or leading—used by economists to permit examination of the overall trend of the particular group of indicators, since these rarely if ever, all move in the same direction. Diffusion indexes are useful predictive devices because they usually reach their highs and lows before the peaks and troughs are reached in the business cycle. (See Index Number.)

**Economic Life** — The period during which an economic good may be profitably utilized; period during which a building or other tool is more valuable in use than for salvage.

**Economics** — The study of man's efforts to allocate limited resources and to produce and exchange the things he needs and wants for his material welfare.

**Economist** — An individual who specializes in the study, formulation, and application of economic theory to the economic life of man.

**Economy** — Originally from a Greek word meaning housekeeping. In modern usage it means man's material welfare, how he produces and exchanges. There are, therefore, several types of economies whose basic differences result from a difference in who owns and directs the tools of production, and who allocates the limited economic resources.

Also used to indicate an instance of thrift or of cost-saving, as in "effecting an economy in production."

**Elasticity of Demand** — See Law of Supply and Demand.

**Entrepreneur** — A person who sees a demand for a good or service and organizes a business enterprise to meet that demand.

**Equipment Trust Certificate** — A type of security, generally issued by a railroad, to pay for new equipment. Title to the equipment, such as a locomotive, is held by a trustee until the notes are paid off.

**Equity** — The ownership interest of common and preferred stockholders in a company. Also, that portion of a mortgaged property or good or service purchased on the installment payment plan that the nominal owner has amortized or paid for.

TOTAL ASSETS
— TOTAL LIABILITIES
= EQUITY

Equity

**Escrow** — A written document or agreement adopted by two parties and placed in the hands of a third party for safekeeping and deliverance upon the fulfillment of some condition or the occurrence of some event as agreed to by the two parties. Cash, deeds, or bonds are often placed in escrow.

**Estimated Current Dividend Yield** — An estimate of the total cash dividends to be declared by a company in the next twelve months divided by the recent price of a share of stock.

**Eurodollars** — American dollars offered to buyers in non-American financial markets, principally in Europe, hence the terms "Eurodollars" and "Euromarkets." Deposit of dollars in foreign institutions and the holding of them by individuals and institutions and by foreign central banks as reserve currencies.

**Excise Tax** — A tax levied upon some phase of the production and distribution of goods and services. The term is sometimes applied to custom duties.

**Expropriation** — The exercise of the soverign right of a government to appropriate private property for public or other use; for example, where a row of houses is acquired under *eminent domain* to extend a street or to put together parcels of land for urban redevelopment programs. Normally, compensation is extended to existing owners, but expropriation has occurred without compensation or with inadequate compensation. (See Nationalization.)

**Fabianism** — A form of socialism based upon the principles of the Fabian Society of Great Britain. Although influenced by Marx, Fabian principles derive mainly from the writings of such economists as John Stuart Mills. Unlike Marxists, Fabians view the government as a social mechanism to be used to promote social welfare rather than a "class organ" to be overthrown, and they favor bringing about socialism through democratic means. Nevertheless, as do Marxists, Fabians advocate a strong central government controlling the tools of production and distributing shares of output according to the needs of individuals rather than their contributions to production.

**Face Value** — The principal value stated on a stock, bond, or other financial instrument. The legal tender value of a token, coin, or other piece of money. Face value is not necessarily an indication of market value. (See Market Value.)

**Factor of Production** — (See Production.)

**Fascism** — A totalitarian, collectivistic political, economic, and social system that exaggerates nationalism and places extreme emphasis on the supremacy of the state. The ownership of the means of production remains in private hands but is subject to extensive control by government. Benito Mussolini brought Fascism to Italy after World War I, and it was later adopted in Germany under Adolph Hitler and called Nazism.

**Featherbedding** — A labor union practice whereby, through its work rules, a labor union requires an employer to assign more workers to a given task than is necessary or to maintain jobs obsoleted by advancing technology, such as insisting upon a "fireman" in diesel-powered locomotives.

**Federal Appropriation** — A financial authorization by the United States Congress to be spent for a specific purpose, such as the annual operating budget for a Federal agency.

**Fee Simple** — A term for the entire estate that an owner is unconditionally and absolutely entitled to dispose of during his life or, should he die without a will, that goes to his heirs and legal representatives.

**Fiat Money** — Inconvertible paper money or money that is not backed up by gold or silver reserves, also called token money. Government declares this money legal tender. (See Legal Tender.)

**Fiduciary** — An individual in a position of special trust and confidence. For example, he may be a trustee responsible for supervising and administering the affairs or funds of another.

**Finance** — The study or the management of the use of funds by business, government, and individuals. The system by which the income of a company is raised and administered. Also the act of conducting financial operations or the furnishing of money.

**Fineness** — The amount of pure gold or silver in bullion or a coin. It is expressed as parts, percentages or carats. For example, silver bullion of .999 fineness means that 99.9% of the total weight of the bullion is pure silver.

**Fiscal Policy** — The conduct of a nation's financial affairs other than those associated with management of the nation's money supply, which is conducted by the Federal Reserve System in the United States. All activities of the Treasury and expenditures authorized by the Congress and conducted by the executive branch fall under Fiscal Policy. Fiscal and monetary policy are not formally coordinated in the United States, thus they often work at cross-purposes, that is, the Federal Reserve System can be pursuing a "tight money" policy to hold down growth in the money supply while the Congress is voting increased expenditures, even deficit spending, which tends to increase the money supply. (See Monetary Policy.)

**Fiscal Year** — A period of twelve consecutive months established by a business or government for accounting purposes, such as budgeting, planning, and financial reporting. An example of fiscal-year would be from June 1, 1974 to May 31, 1975. A calendar-year runs from January 1 to December 31 of the same year.

**Fixed Charges** — A company's expenses, such as bond interest, that it has agreed to pay whether or not earned, which are deducted from income before earnings on equity capital are computed.

**Floating-Rate Notes** — Notes issued by bank holding companies with maturities of 15-25 years and usually at $1,000 and $5,000 values. Of recent origin, these notes pay 1 percentage point above the average rate on 3-month United States Treasury bills, calculated semi-annually, hence the "Floating-Rate" designation. A form of indexing; see indexing.

**Foreign Exchange** — The process of settling debts between establishments or persons in different countries. Also the negotiable monetary instruments used in settling such debts, such as drafts or bills of exchange. The transactions are handled by banks engaged in international operations.

**Foreign Rate of Exchange** — The rate at which the money of one country can be exchanged for the money of another country. Unless governments interfere, the rate of exchange is largely determined by the amount of goods and services that the money of the various countries will buy within those countries. If the productivity of a given country goes down or prices within that country go up, the money of that country will be less desirable, and its rate of exchange with other currencies will go down. After World War II, exchange rates were set by agreement between governments, with the goal of stabilizing world market prices to facilitate foreign trade. Since it might take months for goods to reach the customer in a foreign country, sellers could suffer losses if the value of that country's currency dropped between the time of the sale agreement and of payment for the goods. But since exchange rates were fixed, the only way a country could bring its currency back into realistic exchange ratios with other currencies if its own money lost value would be to devaluate. This also creates chaos in world trade, and since 1973, currencies have been allowed to "float" within prescribed limits, restoring some of the natural adjustments of supply and demand.

**Franchise** — (Business) A special privilege granted by a private corporation to another corporation, allowing the latter to handle the former's products or services under certain agreed-to conditions.

(Government) The right of a citizen to vote. A special privilege granted by a government to an individual or corporation to operate some business as a public service, such as a bus line.

**Free and Open Market** — A market in which supply and demand are expressed without restraint in terms of price. Contrast with a controlled market in which supply, demand and price may all be regulated.

**Free Economy** — An economic system that is based upon the principles of private enterprise. It is characterized by the private ownership of the tools of production; the individual's right to invest, to freely enter into contracts, to take a risk, and to earn a profit, and by a minimum of governmental restrictions on the economy. (See Free Enterprise.)

**Free Enterprise** — An economic system where private business produces goods and provides services to satisfy consumer demands. All of these goods and services are freely exchanged in a competitive marketplace mostly with but sometimes without profit. Government controls on the direction of the economy are minimal.

**Free Trade** — A situation in international trade where the goods of each country are allowed to be traded worldwide without restrictions, such as import tariffs, import or export quotas, import or export licenses, or exchange controls, and without export subsidies by governments of the trading nations.

**Funded Debt** — Usually interest-bearing bonds of a company. Could include long-term bank loans. Does not include short-term loans, preferred or common stock.

**Fungible** — A term used to describe a commodity or service whose individual units are so similar that one unit of the same grade can be interchanged with another unit of the same grade. Fungibles such as wheat, sugar, tin, and money are used to satisfy contractual obligations by agreed-upon quantities rather than in unique, specified units. In manufacturing or assembly, fungible is used to describe products with interchangeable parts, components, or sub-assemblies.

**Futures** — A contract used in trading on the commodity exchange or in the purchase or sale of foreign currency. A futures contract provides for the future delivery of a commodity or foreign currency at a price determined in the present. (See Hedging.)

**G.T.C. Order** — "Good Till Cancelled." A customer's order to his broker to buy or sell at a specified price until the order is either executed or cancelled.

**Gilt-Edged** — High-grade bond issued by a company that has demonstrated its ability to earn a comfortable profit and meet its obligations without interruptions. (See Blue Chip.)

**Gold Certificates** — United States paper currency issued by the United States Treasury Department that is backed or fully secured by gold bullion to the full amount of the certificate. Gold Certificates were in general circulation from 1865 to 1933; after that, they were issued in revised form only to Federal Reserve banks for reserve purposes, and for transfering balances among the seven Federal Reserve districts. Transfers of these reserve certificates were handled through an interdistrict settlement fund, essentially a bookkeeping arrangement, from 1933 until 1973 when gold standard requirements were eliminated.

**Gold Standard** — A monetary system that uses a fixed amount of gold as the standard of value for its monetary unit. In the past, nations on the gold standard usually circulated and made gold coins legal tender at a fixed value, and also issued gold certificates or "paper money" redeemable at their face value in gold. These certificates were the predominant form of legal tender. Since governments on the gold standard had to be prepared to exchange gold for the paper money or certificates, this limited the volume of paper money that could be issued.

**Good Will** — The value of a business in terms of customer attitude and willingness to return to that business for goods and services. It is made up of such intangibles as a business' reputation, trade names, public relations, and drawing power. The actual value of good will is difficult to verify, but it is still often considered a business asset when a business liquidates or is sold.

**Government Bonds** — Obligations of the U.S. Government, regarded as the highest grade because interest and principal can be paid out of taxes.

**Gratuity** — A gift, donation or other voluntary payment given in return for some service rendered. A tip from a customer to a waiter in a restaurant is a gratuity. The word TIP is an acronym for "To Insure Promptness."

**Gross National Product** — A comprehensive barometer of the market value of a nation's total output of goods and services used to measure the general business and economic activity of a nation. It includes both domestic and foreign investment and only the final goods and services before deductions of depreciation charges and other allowances for capital consumption are made.

**Growth Stock** — Stock of a company with prospects for strong future growth, but usually not for immediate profit. It is generally held in anticipation of capital gain rather than for dividends.

**Guaranteed Bond** — A bond for which interest or principal, or both, are guaranteed by a company other than the issuer. Also called an assumed or an indorsed bond.

**Guaranteed Stock** — Usually preferred stock on which dividends are guaranteed by another company.

**Guaranty** — A contract in which a third party, the guarantor, promises to make good in the event of failure of the obligated party to an agreement to satisfy the debt or to perform the specified duty.

**Hard Cash or Hard Money** — Metal coins, such as gold or silver, in contrast to paper money. Also refers to a nation's monetary unit that maintains stable value both domestically and in foreign exchange markets.

**Hedging** — A technique used to minimize price fluctuations in commodity foreign exchange and securities markets between the time a commodity, foreign exchange, or block of securities are bought and the time when they are sold. To hedge, the company sells a future delivery promise of the same amount of the commodity, foreign exchange, or securities as it holds, timing the "futures" contract to the time the holdings will be sold. It then buys in the later market to fulfill its "futures" contract. If prices have risen, it makes up in the value of its in-house holdings what it loses in buying in the higher later market and delivering at the lower futures contract price. If prices decline, it makes up the loss in in-house value by the difference between the lower price it pays in the market to fulfill the futures contract made at the old, higher price. Hedging thus eliminates both risk of loss and possibility of gain; the company does this to permit more or less stable cost budgeting, leaving risk-taking to speculators. The company, consequently, can focus on making its profit in its own business without taking on the risk of a "sideline business," namely, speculation in commodities, foreign exchange, or securities.

**Holding Company** — A corporation that purchases and owns the majority of stock of another corporation or group of corporations in order to control them. A holding company may be formed to just control other companies, or it may be a holding-operating company, which is both a holding company and a company engaged in another business of its own.

**Human Energy** — Man applying his muscular and mental abilities to overcome some type of resistance and perform work. To live, man applies his human energy to natural resources with the aid of tools to change the form, condition, or place of natural resources. For example, human energy, with the aid of tools applied to wood and other materials, provides shelter.

Human Energy

**Hypothecation** — The pledging and depositing of securities or other properties as collateral to secure a loan. From Greek, Hypo-, "under," "beneath."

**Incidents of Ownership** — The power or legal authority to exercise any of the rights and privileges incident to any tangible or intangible property interests. For example, in an insurance policy incidents of ownership include the right to change beneficiaries, withdraw cash values, make loans on the policy, and assign it. These rights may be exercised by the beneficial owner, or by assignment or original purchase to the beneficiary or an assignee who is not the beneficiary.

**Income** — Generally, all money received by an individual or business. In investment, the dividends or interest earned on an investment by an individual or business.

Income before operating expenses are deducted is gross income. Income after operating expenses are deducted but before taxes are deducted, is gross profit. Gross profit, when taxes are deducted, becomes net profit. Profit, while not a fixed expense, must be collected from the customer on behalf of the stockholders whose investment makes the company possible.

**Income Bond** — Generally income bonds promise to repay principal but to pay interest only when earned. An income bond may also be issued as a substitute for preferred stock.

**Income Property** — Property from which income is derived, including commercial rentals and business profits from real estate other than rents.

**Income Statement** — A summary statement showing the amount that a business received during a given period of time. how it was distributed over the various costs of the business, and an indication of the profit or loss position of the business during the time period covered by the income statement.

**Incumbrance** — Any claim, right to or interest in property, such as unpaid tax claims, that depreciates its value to the owner, but does not deprive him of the title nor the power to sell or transfer it.

**Indenture** — An agreement under which bonds or debentures are issued, specifying maturity date, interest rate, security and other terms.

**Index Number** — A number showing ratio of relative change, used in economics as a statistical method for keeping an easily observed running record of important business trends in such things as prices, employment, and unfilled orders. Every index has a base year, which, for comparison purposes, is given the value of 100. If the activity involved in the first year subsequent to the base year increases 10%, the index number rises to 110. Through an index, statisticians, economists and others can evaluate trends and project probable developments. (See Economic Indicator.)

**Indexing** — A "monetary correction" technique first used in Brazil to combat the stultifying effects of runaway inflation on sales of government bonds. Even at high interest rates, investors lost more in purchasing power than they received in interest. Then in 1963, the Brazilian state of

Guanabara began issuing 2 and 5 year bonds with a relatively low interest rate—4 per cent—but with interest calculated on face value, which was adjusted every 3 months in proportion to changes in the nation's general price index. Thus protected against inflation losses, investors immediately began purchasing the bonds. While a palliative rather than a cure for inflation, indexing restored a semblance of order to Brazil's economy and subsequently was extended throughout the economy to include taxes, bank deposits, mortgage loans, wages, rents, and corporate balance sheets. In theory, indexing works to perserve real incomes and purchasing power. It also would "deflate" the nation's currency should the general price index drop, although that has not happened and does not seem likely, given the "inflation psychology" it helps foster. Since indexing has the effect of building inflation—which by definition means the erosion of purchasing power—into the economy, it is difficult to see how indexing can do more than alleviate some of its worst effects in the long run.

"Floating rate notes" are a form of indexing. (See Floating rate notes.)

**Indirect Exchange** — The process of relinquishing one commodity or service for another with the intention of using it to acquire yet other ones. Most often, this takes the form of exchanging goods or services for money, which is then used to purchase the desired commodities or services. Indirect exchange is basic to any money-based economy.

**Individualism** — A political-economic belief that all of the people are better off when each individual is free to do the things that he believes to be in his best interests and in those of his family. In theory, the intervention of government is limited to such things as public works, education, law enforcement, and national defense. In practice, government must also give financial aid to those people incapable of supporting themselves. (See antonym, Collectivism.)

**Industrial Union** — A labor union that generally includes all workers of a particular factory, industry, or group of industries without regard to a worker's specific craft or level of skill. (See Craft or Trade Union.)

**Inflation** — A condition under which the amount of currency in circulation increases faster than the supply of goods and services, resulting in large and rather sudden increases in the general price level and a concomitant decline in the purchasing power of the monetary unit. A "normal" increase in the price level following a period of depression is generally regarded as a price recovery rather than inflation. (See antomym, Deflation.)

**Insolvency** — The inability of a business to pay its debts as they come due. Under Federal Bankruptcy law, the condition in which the liabilities of an individual or organization exceed the realizable value of the assets available for settlement of those liabilities. (See Bankruptcy and antonym, Solvency.)

**Installment** — The partial payment on the purchase price of a good or service, or part payment on a note or tax assessment. In installment buying the thing purchased is sold under an agreement that the purchaser make a specified initial downpayment and then make the remaining payments on specified future dates until full payment of principal, interest, late payment penalties, and other charges are made. Installment buying is buying on credit.

Insurance

**Insurance** — The elimination of, or protection against, risk. This is done when an individual or business concern, the insured, secures a contract with a party, the insurer, who agrees to indemnify the individual, business or other identified beneficiaries should they suffer losses stipulated in the contract. The insured pays a premium to the insurer for this protection. Types of insurance include: life, health, and accident.

**Intangibles** — In accounting, an intangible is a current asset with no material substance, such as good will, patents, trademarks, copyrights. Intangibles are often written off through depreciation or amortization.

In property, an intangible is something of value with no material substance, such as ownership of a bond, stock, or an insurance policy.

**Intangibles Per Share** — A measurement showing the relationship between a company's intangible assets, such as good will and patents, and common shares outstanding. It is computed by dividing the company's intangible assets by the number of common shares outstanding at year end.

**Interest** — A monetary charge by a lender to a borrower for the use of money. It is expressed as a rate or percentage of the amount of money borrowed. For example, if the interest rate is 5% on a $100.00 loan, the interest would be $5.00 (simple interest).

**Inventories** — The supply of various unsold goods in various stages of manufacture and raw materials that a company keeps on hand to meet production and customer needs as they arise. Inventories are also kept on hand to help insure the uninterrupted operation of a business. In statistical reporting, inventories are normally reported in terms of dollar valuation.

Inventories

**Inventory Turnover** — A figure arrived at by dividing a company's sales for a given period, usually a year, by the cost of the average inventory carried during that period. This figure helps to determine the size of inventory a company may need for the following year, and also indicates how efficiently a company is managing its inventory.

**Investment** — The use of money for the purpose of making more money, to gain income or increase capital, or both. (See Speculation.)

**Investment Trust** — A company that uses its capital to invest in other companies.

**Investor** — An individual who exchanges money for some form of income-producing property, normally expected to be held over a considerable period of time. Investors are risk-takers, even though the risk may be very slight. They are the people responsible for the capital accumulation that provides the tools of production.

In the securities market, an individual whose principal concerns in the purchase of a security are regular dividend income, safety of the original investment, and, if possible, capital growth. Contrasts with speculator, whose principal concern is to make money on changes in the market prices of securities.

**Invoice** — An itemized bill compiled by a seller and given to a purchaser, listing the particulars of a sale. This includes: the seller and purchaser; discounts if any; and, the prices, quantities and description of the goods sold.

**Issue** — The selling of bonds, stocks, or other securities by a corporation, which become part of that corporation's debt or obligation. The government making currency available for circulation, or government selling bonds or certificates that become part of the national debt.

**Keynesian Economics** — An economic theory developed by an English economist, John Maynard Keynes, that led to the conclusion that consumption is relatively stable and investment is relatively volatile, so variations in a nation's overall investment level are largely responsible for variations in national income, that is, for prosperity or for "hard times." This, in turn, led to the conclusion that government could act as a compensating factor by influencing investment levels. In recessions, the government would spend more than it takes in in taxes—it would engage in deficit spending, i.e., be an investor. In times of high prosperity when full productive capacity is approached and inflation threatens, it should collect more than it spends and run a surplus, i.e., be a saver. He argued not for direct governmental intervention, but for compensatory fiscal policy; he strongly believed in allowing free markets to determine prices and to allocate resources. Subsequent experience indicates that consumption is not as stable as Keynes thought, lessening the theory's utility as an analytic tool, and that governments tend to follow Keynesian precepts during slow-downs, but ignore them during overexpansion, so the net effect is always inflationary.

Before his death, Keynes reportedly criticized the use of his theory as "a one way street," in that it was used to justify deficits but not surpluses. (See synomyn, New Economists and antonym, Monetarists.)

**Labor** — Generally, the human energy that is directed toward the production of goods and services. Also, all persons who work for a living. In its present economic and sociological meaning, those workers who are members of labor unions, as distinguished from other employees and the employers who are not members of a union. The word "labor" has almost come to be a synonym for the phrase "organized labor."

**Laissez Faire** — "Without interference," or "allow to do." An economic philosophy that originated among the Physiocrats in France in the early 1700's and was made popular by the eighteenth century English economist, Adam Smith. It held that government should only maintain law and order and not regulate the economy.

**Law of Diminishing Returns** — A concept originally developed in relation to land use by the "Classical Pessimist," Thomas Robert Malthus in support of his famous Malthusian Doctrine that population growth would keep wages at or near subsistence level. Further developed by Economist David Ricardo, who systematized Malthus' "Iron Law of Wages," the Law of Diminishing Returns indicates that while initial additional increments of labor and fertilizer will increase yields, further additional units will not proportionately increase the output, and carried far enough, will reduce it.

The Law of Diminishing Returns has subsequently been applied to manufacturing and other economic activities, and while some assumptions about the nature of "fixed" and "variable" production factors have changed, the "law" is generally accepted as valid. Among other things, it now implies that continued increases in farm yield or manufacturing output requires the input of new "variables" such as improved tools and techniques.

**Law of Supply and Demand** — A term used to describe the mechanism that determines the price of any given product in the marketplace at any given time. Both components can be expressed in terms of "schedules" and plotted as lines or curves on a graph. The point at which the line representing *demand* intersects the line representing *supply* is called the equilibrium point, and represents the price at which the supply exactly matches the demand at any given time. Under the concept, supply and demand will always tend to move toward the equilibrium point. If demand increases or the supply is curtailed—a disastrous wheat crop, for example—the price normally will rise until a new equilibrium point (price) is reached. If demand decreases or the supply increases, prices normally will fall until a new equilibrium point is reached. The "shape" of the demand curve as plotted on the graph also is important: if the curve is steep, demand is "inelastic," that is, demand remains pretty much the same regardless of price—salt or food (but not all types of food), since each human must have both. If the curve slopes gradually, it is "elastic," and small price changes either way will greatly increase or decrease purchases—for example, so-called luxury items. "Shifts" in either demand or supply—people tire of hoolahoops, or makers find a new, less expensive way of producing an item and can sell it for less, or it becomes more expensive to produce—also change the intersection point and thus the price.

The "Law of Supply and Demand" is at the core of the self-adjusting mechanism of the competitive free enterprise system, and best meets the needs of the people—that is fulfills their wishes as expressed in their marketplace demands—when given free play. The results of the interplay of supply and demand can be changed by government interference or by private monopolies (organizations that control supply to increase prices and returns), but it still applies, even though taxes, restrictions, allotments, rationing or other devices may be used to establish or to influence the intersection point (price or the balance of supply and demand) rather than the competitive marketplace. These actions obviously frustrate the desires of the people to a greater or lesser extent.

**Lease** — A contract granting to a party the possession and use of land, buildings, machinery, or other specified property for a specific period of time, which may be extended by mutual consent. The party leasing the property pays a sum of money periodically usually called rent, to the owner. The leasing of expensive equipment by business has become popular because it reduces capital expenditures and provides cash flow and other benefits.

**Legal Description** — A statement based on law containing a designation by which land is identified. For example, a title to an owner's piece of property describes the dimensions and exact boundary lines of the property.

**Legal Liability** — Generally, a monetary obligation recognized by the courts and enforceable by law. The owner of a business may have a legal liability to reimburse a customer who may not be satisifed with the performance of a good that the customer bought from the owner.

**Legal List** — A list of investments selected by various states in which certain institutions and fiduciaries, such as insurance companies and banks, may invest.

**Legal Tender** — Money that by law an individual or business is required to accept in payment of a debt or for some good or service.

**Letter of Credit** — A document issued by a bank in which the bank agrees to accept drafts by an individual or business concern that has previously established credit with the bank. The amount of the letter of credit is limited to the credit the individual or business concern has established with the bank. Letters of credit are often used in both domestic and foreign trade.

**Leverage** — A term applied when a company's cost structure is such that the ratio of fixed costs to total costs is high. This produces disproportionately large increases in net income with increases in sales, but also can mean disproportionately sharp drops in net earnings with declines in sales. Also called operating leverage.

Leverage is also used to describe the effect of arranging a company's capital structure so that its capital is largely in the form of fixed commitments such as preferred stock and bonded debt, and common stock accounts for a relatively small proportion of it. In these circumstances, small fluctuations in net income can produce large variations in earnings per share of common stock. Also called capital leverage.

**Liabilities** — The amount of money that a business owes to others. Liabilities include accounts and wages and salaries payable, dividends declared payable, accrued taxes payable, and fixed or long-term liabilities such as mortgage bonds, debentures and bank loans.

**Liberal** — From the Latin word, liber, meaning "free." Broadly defined as connoting generosity, tolerance, broadmindedness, the favoring of reform or progress, not literal or strict. In political-economic use, it formerly was applied to individuals who opposed strong central government; it is now applied to individuals who support the expansion of strong central government and favor extensive welfare programs.

**Lien** — An agreement between parties that allows a creditor to take and keep possession of the property of a debtor until the payment of a debt is made, or the fulfillment of some other obligation is realized.

**Limit Order** — A customer's order to a securities or other broker to buy or sell at a specific price or better. The order can be executed only at that price or a better one.

**Line of Credit** — The maximum amount of credit that an individual or business concern has with a bank; the total amount of money that a person or company can borrow from a bank at any one time. The line of credit can vary, depending on the borrowers' and the bank's financial condition.

**Liquidation** — The process of converting securities or other property into cash. Also, to settle the accounts of a defunct business by disposing of assets to satisfy some portion of debts and obligations.

**Liquidity** — Indicates the relative ease with which an individual or business can convert assets into cash on relatively short notice without appreciable monetary loss. *Liquidity position* indicates whether an individual or business has a relatively high or relatively low proportion of its assets in liquid instruments—cash and notes or other vehicles readily converted into cash—or in frozen or illiquid form. In securities, liquidity refers to the ability of the market to absorb a reasonable amount of buying or selling of a particular stock with only reasonable price changes. A market that cannot do so is said to be "thin." Liquidity is an important characteristic of a good market.

**List Price** — A printed price, as one published in a catalog, that does not include rebates, trade or cash discounts, and commissions. Sometimes called simply "list," which is also a short term used to refer to all listed securities traded on a stock exchange.

**Listed Stock** — The stock of a company that is traded on a national securities exchange, and for which a listing application and a registration statement, giving detailed information about the company and its operations, have been filed with the Securities & Exchange Commission and the exchange itself. (See antonym, Over-the-Counter-Market, and Off-Board.)

**Load Factor** — (Business) The relationship of the demand for a company's product or service to the company's capacity to provide those goods and services. (See Capacity.)

**Locked In** — An investor is said to be locked in when he has a profit on a security he owns but does not sell because his profit would immediately subject him to the capital gains tax.

**Long** — A long buyer in stocks and bonds usually buys expecting the market price to advance. Often he is a Bull on the market and buys on margin. (See Short Sale.)

**Machine Tools** — Machine tools are described as the "mother tools of economic life."

Machine tools make all of the production facilities for manufacturing steel, lumber, petroleum, printing, textiles, etc. Machine tools also mass produce the individual unit parts that are assembled into such things as automobiles, farm machinery, and thousands of devices and appliances we use every day.

A machine tool is defined as: 1. A power driven machine —not portable by hand—that shapes or forms metal by cutting, impact, pressure, electrical techniques or a combination of these processes. 2. That class of machine used to make all other tools including the ability to make other machine tools. 3. Mechanical robots that evolved as extensions of metalworking hand tools. (See chart p. 54-55.)

**Maintenance** — The amount of money required to keep the tools of production in good and usable condition. Maintenance is a charge against current expenses and is part of the first cost. (See Costs.)

**Management** — The Board of Directors, elected by the stockholders, and the officers of the corporation, appointed by the Board of Directors.

**Man's Material Welfare**

**Manipulation** — Buying or selling a security for the purpose of creating false or misleading appearance of active trading or for the purpose of raising or depressing the price.

**Man's Material Welfare** — Every material thing that has an economic value measurable by price and can be bought and sold. Man's material welfare is the product of natural resources plus human energy multiplied by tools. Those men and nations that have more, produce more.

**Margin** — The amount of money paid in on an investment, expressed as a percentage of the current market value of the investment. The balance is advanced by the broker.

**Margin Call** — A demand upon a customer to put up money or securities to strengthen his credit position with the broker.

**Market** — The communication and interaction between the seller and buyer of goods and services. The exchange of goods and services based upon geography, such as local, national, or international markets, or exchange based upon the kinds of items traded, for example, stock, produce or livestock markets. (See Market Place.)

**Market Order** — An order by a customer to a broker to buy or sell at the best price available when the order reaches the trading floor.

**Market Place** — Any place, such as the open space markets of Feudal England or the modern shopping centers of the twentieth century, where goods and services are exchanged between a buyer and a seller. Sometimes used interchangeably with market. (See Market.)

**Market Price** — The price at which anything is currently sold on the open market, or the price at which a seller is willing to sell anything and which the buyer is willing to pay. In the case of a security, market price is usually considered the last reported price.

**Market Value** — The amount that could be obtained for a good or service in a free market, providing the seller and the buyer were fully informed, acted voluntarily, and that rights and benefits inherent in or attributable to the good or service were included in the transfer. Market value connotes the historical, estimated, or usual value of a good or service, but what the good or service is or can be sold for at any given time, is the market price. Market value and market price may, therefore, not always coincide.

**Marketing** — All business activities directed toward and resulting in the flow of goods and services from the producer to the consumer. Marketing includes: researching consumer preferences, packaging, pricing, promoting, distributing, and often service obligations. Also used to describe basic management functions narrowly centered on market research, study of unfilled consumer needs and development of new products to meet those needs, and introductions and promotions of the new products.

**Mark-up** — The difference between the amount that a business pays for something and the amount for which it is sold.

**Marxism** — The teachings of Karl Marx and Friedrick Engels, which serve as the basis for Bolshevism and many forms of socialism.

**Materialism** — A term applied to individuals who value material things and wealth over spiritual or intellectual pursuits. Also a doctrine that asserts that all change is brought about by material things or events, and thus all human values and ideas can be reduced to material causes and matters.

**Mathematical Simulation** — A computer-based analytical technique used by businesses and other organizations to study the probable results of various kinds of decisions including pricing, introduction of new products, and capital investment, under varying possible conditions. The technique not only helps indicate what is likely to happen under each set of circumstances but also can provide an estimate of the risk involved in each, helping management to formulate policies and make prudent decisions.

**Maturity** — The date on which the principal of a full term loan or a bond or debenture comes due and must be paid off.

**Mercantilism** — A term applied by critics to a body of economic thought that emerged in Europe after the Middle Ages. It never achieved the coherence of a system, but its concepts found wide acceptance in the 16th and 17th centuries. Proponents argued that a nation's power and wealth lay in its holdings of precious metals. Products and services were not true wealth, but could be used to obtain it. Thus, they favored steps designed to promote exports and curtail imports, hoping to achieve a "favorable balance of trade" that would bring in gold and silver — a precept that lingers on today. Adam Smith and later critics argued that the real power and strength of a nation lies in its production and its productivity. Where "mercantilists" believed one nation's gain was another nation's loss, the critics held that trade is profitable to all trading nations. Consequently, they espoused free trade and decried protectionism, arguing that obviously every nation cannot enjoy a "favorable balance of payments" and that efforts to do so invited retaliation and worked to reduce productivity and to retard the growth of real wealth worldwide. England adopted many of the new ideas and prospered; Spain, endowed with the rich mines of the new world, clung to mercantilism and went into gradual economic decline. (See: Productivity, Protectionism.)

**Merger** — The combination of two or more business enterprises with the dominant enterprise absorbing the assets and liabilities of the other business concern or concerns. After a merger, all business enterprises usually operate as a division of, or under the name of the dominant enterprise.

**Middleman** — A term applied to a business engaged exclusively in the distribution of products or commodities from the producer to the consumer. Middlemen do not change the form or condition of the goods they handle. They merely take part in the exchange process. Middlemen may be wholesalers, retailers, distributors, jobbers, or brokers.

**Militarism** — A policy of aggressive military preparedness. Also, a political, social, and economic system that is controlled by and operated in the interests of the military rather than civilian population. Nazi Germany was a militaristic society.

**Mint** — A government-owned building where bullion—ingots of silver or gold—is made into metallic money for legal tender. Coins may be "full-bodied" (contain metal equivalent to face value) or "token." Privately-owned mints normally produce medallions and special non-monetary commemorative coins but may be commissioned by government to produce monetary coins.

**Minutes** — A written record of what occurred during a meeting of an organization. Generally, corporation charters require that minutes of a stockholders or board of directors meeting be recorded and kept. Meeting rules of order normally require that these minutes be read at the beginning of the next meeting, although that is often waived.

**Monetarists** — Term applied to economists and others who espouse the precepts of the quantity theory of money, which implies greater stress on monetary than on fiscal policy. Adherants of the other major school of economic thought are variously called "fiscalists" or new economists; their approach is based on Keynesian economics and stresses fiscal over monetary policy. Both schools agree that both monetary and fiscal considerations are relevant, but differ strongly on their relative importance. Monetarists hold that changes in the money supply have a larger, more predictable, and quicker impact upon the economy than do fiscal or government spending and taxing policies, and, in fact, argue that fiscal change is not an important factor affecting aggregate demand. Most monetarists, consequently, argue that a steady policy of moderate monetary stimulus consistent with long run growth needs of the economy will produce steadier growth and greater economic stability than an activist policy of "fine tuning" via fiscal means. Fiscalists disagree. (See antonym, New Economists.)

**Monetary Base** — A figure computed by the Federal Reserve and published weekly that can be used to discern some of the effects of monetary actions by the "Fed" upon economic activity and financial markets. It is computed by summing member bank deposits and currency held by both banks and others, and adding reserves, adjusted for legal and other changes to maintain comparability over time.

**Monetary Policy** — The management of a nation's money supply, normally conducted by a Central Bank—in the United States, by the Federal Reserve System. Established by an Act of Congress signed by the President in December of 1913, the Federal Reserve System is not a single centralized institution, but rather consists of 12 regional "banker's banks" that function with a considerable degree of autonomy within their regions, although overall policy is coordinated through the Federal Open Market Committee. The Federal Reserve System "manages" the nation's money supply basically by buying and selling securities, thus inserting funds into, or removing them from circulation, by changing bank reserve requirements, thus making more or less funds available for lending, and by changing the discount rate or the interest rate banks pay to borrow funds from the Federal Reserve System, thus making it cheaper or more expensive to borrow those funds to cover loans to bank customers. The "Fed" does not have a direct voice in "Fiscal Policy," which may or may not be in concert with Monetary Policy. (See Fiscal Policy.)

**Money** — Historically, anything that is generally accepted in exchange for other things, namely, economic goods, which include services. In modern societies, money takes the form of cash—paper certificates and coins issued by the monetary authorities, which are "legal tender"—plus checks and other negotiable instruments. All sorts of items ranging from "Wampum" (Indian shell beads) through carved stones, furs, and tobacco have been used as money.

**Money Purchase Plan** — A plan to apply periodically a fixed amount of money to purchase an annuity that may makeup all or a portion of a retirement pension.

**Monopoly** — From the Greek word, *Monos,* "one" plus *polein,* "sell." The almost absolute control by a single seller over the production, pricing, and distribution of a single good or service, or group of goods and services. A seller with a monopoly either has no or very little competition. Private monopolies are owned and controlled by an individual or business, although "natural monopolies," such as utilities, usually are regulated by government. Public monopolies, such as the Post Office, are controlled by government. Monopoly is sometimes loosely used to describe combinations in restraint of trade instead of the more precise terms, Cartel and Oligopoly (*Oligos,* "few" plus "sell"). (See antonym, Competition.)

**Monopsony** — One buyer. Like monopoly (one seller), monopsony tends to restrict output. The same firm can be both a monopolist in the market it sells in, and a monopsonist in the market it buys in. Can be established by a government, i.e., when the United States Government made the Atomic Energy Commission sole legal customer for domestic uranium ore. (See antonym, Competition.)

**Mortgage** — A written and legal transfer of title to property from a debtor to a creditor. However, it is not a transfer of possession of property from a debtor to a creditor. The title to property is returned to the debtor once he has made full payment for the property to the creditor. It is different from a lien in that in a mortgage the creditor has title to the property.

**Mortgage**

**Mortgage Bond** — A bond secured by a mortgage on a property. The market value of the property may or may not equal the value of the mortgage.

**Mortgage Certificate** — An interest in a mortgage evidenced by a document that sets forth the terms of an agreement, such as the principal and the amount, date, and place of payment. The parties to the agreement are the mortgagees who hold the certificates and the mortgagor. Unlike bonds or notes, mortgage certificates entail no obligation to pay money. Certificates are merely a certification by the mortgage holder that he holds the mortgage for the benefit and in the interest of the certificate holders.

**Mortgagee** — The individual or company that is the source of funds or the creditor for a mortgage loan. Generally, a bank or a savings and loan association is the mortgagee for a mortgage loan on a home or building for a business.

**Mortgagor** — The individual or company who has all or some part of the title to property and by written agreement pledges that property as security for a debt. For example, a man who buys a house and mortgages that house through a bank is the mortgagor. In effect the mortgagor is the debtor and the bank is the creditor until the mortgage is paid in full.

**Most-Favored-Nation-Clause** — A clause in a commercial agreement or treaty between two nations binding the nations to guarantee to each other all favorable foreign trade concessions granted in the future by either nation to another country.

**Motion** — A formal proposal, usually verbal, to bring any subject up before an assembly. A motion may be seconded, discussed, added to, and voted on by those in the assembly. It begins with the words, "I move that." For example, motions are made in stockholders and board of directors meetings to vote on the acceptance of a report, to appoint new officers, to adopt a policy, to make merger decisions, or to adjourn the meeting.

**Multinational Company** — A company that has at least one manufacturing or distribution facility in a foreign country. A multinational company conducts its business functions and activities with a worldwide perspective.

**Municipal Bond** — A bond issued by a state or a political subdivision, such as county, city, town or village. The term also designates bonds issued by state agencies and authorities. In general, interest paid on municipal bonds is exempt from Federal income taxes, making them attractive to investors in high income brackets despite their low interest rates, and making it possible for municipalities to obtain "cheap money."

**Mutual Fund** — An investment company that does not have a fixed amount of capital stock, but continuously sells shares in itself to the public. The funds from selling shares in itself are pooled by the mutual fund and invested in securities, such as common stocks or bonds. If the Mutual Fund makes money from its investments, the investors in the fund are then paid dividends on their investments.

**National Debt** — The total indebtedness of a national government to individuals, institutions, and foreign governments. Interest must be calculated and paid on the national debt. A rising national debt can contribute significantly to inflation, especially if significant portions of it are based upon the creation of new money—deficit spending—rather than consisting of existing "earned" money borrowed from the private sector.

**Nationalization** — The process by which a national government takes over total control of a business or an industry previously owned and operated by private citizens. (See Expropriation.)

Natural Resources

**Natural Resources** — Natural Resources are all the things made by nature and are one of the key factors in the production of goods and services. To have food, clothing and shelter, man must diligently apply his physical and mental energies with the aid of tools to the changing of natural resources in their form, condition or place. Some nations, such as Brazil and the United States, have large amounts of natural resources. Brazilians, however, do not enjoy material welfare comparable to that enjoyed by Americans because Brazilians do not presently have the technical skills or tools to change significantly their natural resources into the necessities and comforts of life. The Arab states are wisely beginning to trade large amounts of their chief natural resource, oil, not only for consumer goods, but also for the technical skill and the tools of production that help them to increase their material welfare. Prosperous nations, such as Japan and Switzerland, who have limited natural resources, have either capitalized on their natural scenery to build a strong tourism industry, or have traded and sold their technical skills and tools to acquire the natural resources of other countries.

**Negotiable** — Refers to a security, title to which, when properly endorsed by the owner, is transferable by delivery.

**Net Asset Value** — A term usually used in connection with investment trusts, meaning net asset value per share.

**Net Change** — The change in the price of a security from the closing price on one day and the closing price on the following day on which the stock is traded.

**Net Income** — A business' revenues that are left after all operating costs, including taxes, have been paid for a given period. Net income can be paid to the stockholders as a dividend or reinvested back into the company. Generally, net income is synonymous with net earnings.

**Net Lease** — A lease requiring the lessee to assume payment of all property operating expenses, such as insurance, taxes, and maintenance, in addition to the payment of rent.

**Net Plant** — The total monetary worth of a company's plant, equipment and land, at the land's original cost, less accumulated reserves for depreciation.

**Net Profits** — Profits remaining from revenues after deducting the cost of the goods sold and all operating costs, including interest, depreciation, and taxes.

**Net Sales** — A company's gross or total sales less returns, discounts, and allowances granted.

**Net Worth** — The tangible assets of a business less its liabilities represents net worth or the owners' equity for credit appraisal purposes. Sometimes a company will include intangible assets, such as patents and goodwill, when computing net worth for the balance sheet.

**New Economists** — A term applied to economists and others who espouse an activist approach to "fine tuning" of the economy by means of both fiscal and monetary policies, but with by far greater stress upon changes in fiscal or government spending and taxing policies. This "New Economics" is largely based on Keynesian concepts. In general new economists or "fiscalists," as they are sometimes called, believe autonomous investment expenditures, federal tax, and federal expenditure policies exert a major influence on private spending decisions, and thus, fiscal policy is the major policy tool available for influencing economic activity. Adherants to the other major school of economic thought, who embrace the quantity theory of money and are, consequently, known as "Monetarists," hold the opposite view, and in addition, contend that activist policies tend to disrupt and de-stabilize the economy. (See antonym, Monetarists.)

**New Issue** — A stock or bond sold by a corporation for the first time. Proceeds may be used to retire outstanding securities of the company for new plant or equipment, or for additional working capital.

**Obsolescence** — The loss in value and desirability of an asset or good due to changes or improvements in technology and changes in public preference or demand. Obsolescence may occur even though an asset or good has not physically deteriorated.

**Off-Board** — This term may refer to transactions over-the-counter (O-T-C) in unlisted securities, or in a special situation, to a transaction involving a block of listed shares that was not executed on a national securities exchange. (See Listed Stock and Over-the-Counter-Market.)

**Offer** — The price at which a person is ready to sell.

**Open Order** — An order to buy or sell a security at a specified price. It remains in effect until executed or cancelled by the customer.

**Open Shop** — A factory or other business enterprise that will hire both members and non-members of labor unions. After being hired, the employee is free to join or not join a union. (See antonyms, Agency Shop, Closed Shop and Union Shop.)

**Operating Report** — See Income Statement.

**Option** — A right to buy or sell specific securities or properties at a specified price within a specified time.

**Over-the-Counter-Market** — The market, often termed simply O-T-C, for securities that are not purchased or sold on organized security exchanges. Most government municipal bonds and corporate bonds are sold by the government or corporation issuing the bonds or over-the-counter. (See antonyms, Listed Stock and Off-Board.)

**Overhead** — (Business) See Fixed Costs.

**Overproduction** — A situation in which a business is unable to find customers for all of the goods that it has produced.

**Paper Money** — Any legal money substitute issued by the government and used as money. Paper money has a stated value and may be, but is not always, backed up by reserves of gold and silver. Also called token money as opposed to full-bodied money (i.e., silver dollars, $5 gold pieces).

Paper Money

**Paper Profit** — An unrealized profit on a security still held. Paper profits become realized profits only when the security is sold.

**Par or Parity** — Face or official value. In monetary use, this refers to the established value of a nation's currency vis-a-vis those of other nations, traditionally expressed in terms of a given amount of bullion. Domestically, the amount of gold or silver officially decreed by the government to be the legal equivalent of the nation's monetary unit. (See Par Value.)

**Par Value** — The value of a stock or a bond that is stated on the certificate. Par Value may or may not be the same as the market value.

**Parliamentary Procedures** — A set of formal rules and forty-four parliamentary motions for stockholders or board of directors meetings based upon American Parliamentary Law and Robert's Rules of Order. Parliamentary Procedures seek to protect the rights of the majority, minority, and individuals at a meeting. Even the rights of those absent are safeguarded.

**Participating Preferred Stock** — A type of preferred stock issued by a corporation that entitles the stockholders to share with the common stockholders in additional dividends when a corporation's profits are above a certain amount. These additional dividends would be beyond what normally would be paid to a preferred stockholder.

**Partnership** — A form of business organization where two or more individuals agree to contribute some amount of their property, skill, and labor and share in the risks and profits of the venture. Unlike shareholders in a corporation, any partner may be personally liable for the debts of the partnership. A partnership ends if one of the partners dies, goes bankrupt, or is declared legally insane.

**Passed Dividend** — Omission of a regular or scheduled dividend.

**Patent** — A government grant entitling an inventor or owner of an invention to its exclusive use. In the United States, patent rights expire after 17 years. The holder of a patent is legally entitled to permit others to make use of the patent and to receive payments called royalties.

Patent

**Per Cent Earned on Total Capital** — A figure that shows the percentage a company earned for a given period of time on its total capital. To get this figure, net income plus interest paid on long-term debts is divided by the total capital.

**Per Cent Earned on Net Worth** — A percentage showing the ratio between a company's net income for a given period to its net worth. This figure is computed by dividing the net income by the net worth.

**Percentage Lease** — A commercial lease of property where the rent is based upon a percentage of either the total or a portion of the sales income of the lessee. Thus, when sales are low the rent decreases. As sales increase, the rent increases.

**Petty Cash** — A fund of money that is set apart for the disbursement of cash for petty expenses, such as postage or small supplies. Vouchers are kept for each petty cash disbursement to determine where the money is being spent and who is spending it.

**Petty Cash**

**Point** — In the case of shares of stock, a point means $1. If General Motors shares rise 3 points, each share has risen $3. In the case of bonds a point means $10, since a bond is quoted as a percentage of $1,000.

**Portfolio** — Holdings of securities by an individual or institution.

**Preferred Stock** — A class of stock with a claim on the company's earnings before payment may be made on the common stock and usually entitled to priority over common stock if the company liquidates. Unlike owners of common stock, owners of preferred stock do not have a vote in the management of a company.

**Premium** — The amount of money that an insured party pays either annually or less frequently on an insurance policy. In a gold or silver coin, the difference between the lawful face value of it in paper money and the market value of its metallic content. If the market value of its metallic content is higher, there is a premium, which means more paper money must be paid for the coin.

The difference between the face value of a security and its market value when the market value is higher.

Generally, an increase in value above a given figure, but also a reward or prize extended as an inducement to buy.

**Price** — The value of a good or service stated in money terms for purposes of exchange. The price set by the seller is called the asking price. The price paid by the buyer is called the selling or exchange price, which may or may not be the asking price. Wholesale price is the price asked of a volume or functional middleman; retail price is the price asked of the consumer. The process of establishing a price by examining costs and market demand is called pricing.

**Price Level** — The average exchange price of a selected group of products, commodities, or services at a given time expressed in a composite figure called an index number. The index number can then be compared with index numbers from earlier periods to determine general price level movements. Wholesale and retail price indexes are examples; the consumer price index is a figure derived from a typical mix of products, weighted or adjusted for relative importance.

**Primary Distribution** — Also called primary offering. The original sale of a company's securities. In product marketing, a firm's principal channels of distribution or markets.

**Prime Rate of Interest** — The per cent rate of interest charged by commercial banks for short-term loans to their best customers or customers with the highest credit rating, normally large corporations. The prime rate is the base rate for the rate of interest charged businesses with lower credit ratings and the general public, and is always the "best money price," that is, the lowest rate of interest available for short-term loans.

**Principal** — The par value of a note, stock, bond or the amount of a debt less the interest or premium that the holder is entitled to at maturity. Interest is computed based on the principal. The person for whom a broker executes an order, or a dealer buying or selling for his own account. Also used to refer to a partner or owner in a professional firm, and to a person or firm primarily liable for an obligation, in contrast with an endorser or insurer.

**Production** — The combining of resources, labor and tools to produce real goods. More broadly, production includes services, as in a nation's Gross National Product (its total annual output of goods and services). A Factor of Production is anything that contributes to, or is used in, production. Traditionally, factors of production have been classified in one of three categories: Natural Resources, Human Labor, and Capital Goods. (See Productivity, Gross National Product.)

**Productivity** — The relationship between "output" or the quantity of goods and services produced, and "inputs" or the amounts of labor, material, and capital needed to produce the goods and services. Productivity can be measured in relation to a single input factor or in terms of a "total factor" composite index. Most commonly used is the single factor measure, "output per manhour," because labor is quantitatively the most important input factor in the economy and because output per manhour can be measured relatively quickly and accurately and remains "internally consistent." Composite indices, while theoretically more useful because they also would provide cost information, are difficult and time-consuming to prepare and are not "internally consistent" (their make-up changes with time). Because of the difficulty of identifying and measuring all cost factors, the accuracy of composite indices is questionable, and no generally accepted composite index has yet been developed.

Productivity is the key element that determines the health of a business and in shaping the health of the economy, strongly influencing profitability and the survival probability of the business firm, and determining the nation's level of material welfare. Rising productivity means better pay, increased advancement opportunities, and better profit possibilities for the business firm and all employed by it, and a rising standard of living for the nation's citizens. Static or declining productivity means fewer opportunities for firms and their employees and a declining standard of living for all, since in either case, population growth cannot be accommodated without diverting a portion of existing output to the newcomers.

Since increasing productivity basically means producing more with the same or fewer input factors, it can be fostered by better, more efficient use of resources, improved quality control, elimination of waste, "working smarter," employee work satisfaction and positive attitude, improved design that saves materials or production time, and by the use of new and improved tools. Of these, new improved tools have theoretically and historically proven to be the most vital factor in increasing productivity, both because they produce more and because they help "force" new and improved methods of production. Rising productivity is the prerequisite to an economy capable of providing better opportunities for more people and a higher level of material welfare.

**Profit and Loss** — Profit is the amount of income left after a business pays its bills including operating expenses, production costs, and income taxes. *Gross profit* equals net sales less the cost of goods sold, inventory losses, and in manufacturing firms, factory overhead. *Net profit* is the gross profit less selling and general operating expenses and corporate income taxes. Profits are shared by the owners of a company or reinvested back into the company. Profits vary, and in some years companies do not make a profit. When profits increase, companies can buy more and better tools, provide more and better consumer goods, and pay higher wages to employees. Profits motivate people to invest their savings in business by which everyone can benefit. Loss is the opposite of profit. Loss occurs when a company's operating expenses, income taxes, and other costs exceed its income in a given period of time, for example one year. When a company has a loss, both the firm's owners and employees suffer.

In accounting, profit sometimes is used more broadly to indicate an increase in wealth resulting from the operation of a business.

**Profit Sharing** — A bonus or share of the earnings above their regular wages that employees receive from their employer on an annual or other basis.

**Profit Taking** — Selling to take a profit; the process of converting paper profits on securities that have risen in value since purchase into cash.

**Progressive Income Tax** — An income tax whose rate is higher on the incomes that are higher. For example, a man whose taxable income is $5,000 per year may pay a $1,000 tax (20%), while a man whose taxable income is $50,000 per year may pay a $20,000 tax (40%). The progressive income tax was put into effect by the United States Government in 1914. Many states have also adopted this form of taxation. People who support this tax plan believe that it is bad for the nation for some individuals to receive much more than other individuals. People who oppose progressive income taxation believe that the chance of earning (and keeping) a larger income encourages all the people to do their best and thereby benefits all the people.

**Proletarian** — A member of the working class. Most often used to refer to industrial workers but includes agricultural workers and domestics. Is in distinction to the so-called Bourgeois or merchant class, nobility, landholders, and white collar workers, employers, and management. The term has lost much of its precision with the emergence of modern industrial economies in which blue collar workers often earn more and own more than white collar workers, shopkeepers, and other members of the "Bourgeois."

Promissory Note

**Promissory Note** — A promise in writing by a person to pay a certain sum of money to another at a fixed time, and if appropriate, at a specific interest rate.

**Property** — The exclusive right of an individual to own and control an economic good. Also, the economic good which an individual owns and controls.

Real property is strictly land, including whatever is growing and erected on it and that which is affixed to the structures erected.

Personal property is everything that is not real property including intangibles such as rights and insurance.

**Proprietorship** — A form of business organization where one individual owns the business. Proprietorships are the commonest form of business and are generally small businesses, such as a farm or retail clothing store.

**Prospectus** — A circular that describes securities being offered for sale to the public. Required by the Securities Act of 1933, the prospectus must meet Securities and Exchange Commission standards concerning financial standing, operation, and prospects for the firm making the offer.

**Protectionism** — Describes the policies pursued by national governments that impose legal restrictions on imports to hamper their ability to compete with domestic products. These restrictions take such forms as protective tariffs, embargoes, import quotas, and unreasonable licensing requirements. Subsidies to bolster the competitive position of domestic firms also constitute protectionist measures. These policies hurt domestic producers who sell abroad by making it difficult for foreigners to earn domestic currency to buy from them with, and by inviting retaliatory measures by other governments. (See Free Trade, Tarrif.)

**Proxy** — Written authorization given by a shareholder to someone to represent him and vote his shares at a shareholders' meeting.

**Proxy Statement** — Information required by SEC to be given stockholders as a prerequisite to solicitation of proxies for a listed security.

**Public Affairs** — Programs that a company undertakes to educate government officials about the company's goods and services. Public affairs also involves programs that a company sponsors to inform its employees and/or the general public about some issue or series of issues of public concern.

**Public Relations** — Activities conducted by a company or organization to foster favorable attitudes—good will—towards the company and its products, either among the general public or among members of special groups, such as designers, engineers, purchasing agents, or contractors. "PR" may include direct contact with the public—plant tours, open house—but most efforts are geared to reaching target groups through newspapers, magazines, trade publications, and radio and television. In contrast to advertising, PR exposure in publications or electronic media airtime is not paid for by the firm or organization. PR also includes the sponsoring of charitable or civic events, and the donation of time and money to educational or public service programs. (See Advertising.)

**Pump Priming** — Large scale government spending in such areas as public works, national defense, and farming to stimulate overall business activity.

**Puts and Calls** — Negotiable options that give the right to buy or sell a fixed amount of a certain stock at a specified price within a specified time. A put gives the holder the right to sell the stock; a call the right to buy the stock.

**Quorum** — The number of members of any organized body, such as a board of directors or legislature, that must be present before that body can legally transact business.

**Quotation** — Often shortened to "quote." The highest bid to buy and the lowest offer to sell a security in a given market at a given time.

**Radical** — A person who favors extreme and sometimes violent change in the political, social, and economic structure.

**Reactionary** — In general, anyone who "reacts" against most or all proposed changes in his nation's social, political, and economic structure, or, where change has occurred that he dislikes, advocates a return to the former condition. In this country, it is sometimes used indiscriminately with conservative, but while both strongly support private property rights, the conservative does not resist change as such, but rather insists that its ramifications be carefully thought out, and that it does not erode individual freedom and established rights. Because of this, the conservative generally prefers gradual to radical change.

**Real Money** — Term applied to monetary units with intrinsic or certified value, including full-bodied specie—coins with silver or gold content equivalent to face value—or to monetary units in certificate form that are convertible into silver or gold.

**Real Wages** — Determined by what money received as wages will buy at any given time. Real wages can thus decline with price level rises, or increase with price level declines while money or actual wages remain the same. Money wages can be converted into real wages by the use of index numbers.

**Recession** — A relatively mild, and temporary—usually less than a year in duration—decline in overall business activity not sharp or severe enough to be termed a depression.

**Redemption** — The retirement or payment of debts such as notes and bonds prior to or on the date of maturity. Exchange of currency or monetary certificates for gold by the government that issued the currency as a receipt for a specified amount of gold.

**Redemption Price** — The price at which a bond may be redeemed before maturity, at the option of the issuing company. Redemption value also applies to the price the company must pay to call in certain types of preferred stock.

**Refinancing** — Same as refunding. New bond issues or securities are sold by a company and the money is used to retire older bond issues or existing securities.

**Registered Bond** — A bond registered on the books of the issuing company in the name of the owner. It is a negotiable bond but can be transferred only when endorsed by the registered owner, with the new owner becoming the registered owner.

**Remittance** — Payment in cash or its equivalent, such as a check, for a debt.

**Rental Value** — The amount of money that a tenant or tenants pay or can reasonably be expected to pay for the use of property in a normal rent market. A property's rental value significantly affects its market value.

**Reserves** — (Business) Funds held in cash or liquid (readily converted to cash) instruments, normally earmarked to meet specific costs the business knows it must later meet. (Banking) The portion of total loanable assets a bank holds in cash or liquid form to cope with unusual developments, such as large unexpected withdrawals. Legal reserves are the minimum a bank can keep under law; members of the Federal Reserve System must keep part of these on deposit with their regional Federal Reserve bank (primary reserves) and part on hand (secondary reserves). Banks prefer to hold no more cash than necessary to transact business, since it earns no interest. By changing reserve requirements, by buying or selling securities, and by changing the discount rate—what its member banks pay to borrow funds from it—The Federal Reserve regulates the growth in the nation's money supply.

Free reserves are the total amount of loanable funds commercial banks have on hand, minus any funds borrowed from the Federal Reserve. For any given bank, they represent the difference between the total the bank can legally loan at its current reserve requirement position and what it has actually loaned out, less any funds borrowed at the Federal Reserve discount window.

**Resolution** — A written proposal stating an opinion or resolving that an organization do something. Resolutions are motions put into writing and begin with the word, "Resolved . . .".

**Retail** — The level of business distribution where goods and services are sold to the ultimate consumer, and not for resale. A grocery store that sells food to a family for their own consumption is an example of a retail business. (See Middleman and Wholesale.)

Retail

**Retained Earnings** — Company earnings after taxes and dividends on profit have been paid. Often used as a source of funds for business expansion.

**Revaluation** — The action by which a nation fully or partially restores the value of its depreciated currency, or increases its purchasing power in relation to other currencies. Where money is convertible into gold, this means an increase in the amount of gold a government will extend to redeem its currency. The corollary is that gold costs less in terms of domestic currency, (i.e., it takes fewer domestic monetary units to buy gold). This has the immediate effect of increasing the value (purchasing power) of the nation's currency in relation to currencies of other nations and, by making domestic goods more expensive to foreigners and foreign goods cheaper domestically, tends to encourage imports and discourage exports. Action normally taken when a country's currency is strong vis-a-vis other currencies and the nation is paying too much for imports and not getting "fair value" for its exports. When currency exchange rates change with supply and demand, a nation can also revalue its currency gradually by increasing productivity without increasing the money supply, or by pursuing deflationary policies. (See antonym, Devaluation.)

**Revenue Sharing** — A process by which the Federal government gives back to the states a portion of the income tax revenues that the Federal government collects from the states' citizens and businesses. Local governments are then granted a portion of this money by their respective state. By law, revenue sharing money is either general (money that can be spent for any legitimate purpose) or special (money that must be spent on a program designated by the Federal government).

**"Right" and "Left"** — Terms derived from the seating arrangement of the French Assembly in the late eighteenth century in which the liberal and radical members sat on the left, moderates sat in the center, and monarchists and conservatives sat on the right. In present usage, "right" is used to describe individuals who support limited government, while "left" is used to describe individuals who support expanded government. Naturally, there are gradations within both "left" and "right" parties and groups.

**Rights** — When a company wants to raise more funds by issuing additional securities, it may give its stockholders the opportunity, ahead of others, to buy the new securities in proportion to the number of shares each owns. The piece of paper evidencing this privilege is called a right. Because the additional stock is usually offered to stockholders below the current market price, rights ordinarily have a market value of their own and are actively traded.

**Robert's Rules of Order** — A reference book written by General Henry M. Robert that provides a formal set of rules for orderly meetings. Corporations use Robert's Rules in their stockholder and board of directors meetings. These rules are meant to be only a reference or guide. Thus, in some cases, they may be superseded by a corporation's own formal rules of order for meetings.

**Round Lot** — A unit of trading or a multiple thereof. On the New York Stock Exchange the unit of trading is generally 100 shares in stocks and $1,000 par value in the case of bonds.

**Royalties** — Payments made to the owner of a patent or a copyright; also payments made to the owners of natural resources (such as a forest or mine) in return for permission to use them up.

**Sales Per Share** — A percentage showing the relation between net sales and common shares outstanding. It is computed by dividing net sales at year end by the number of common shares outstanding at year end.

**Script** — A certificate or document indicating that the bearer may exchange it for something. In the past, script has been used to denote fractional paper money issued by a bank or government. Script is a temporary certificate or document and not money. Occasionally, corporations issue script for fractional shares of stock representing dividends that will be deferred to a later date.

**Securities** — Documents evidencing ownership or creditorship in a corporation and establishing a right to receive a payment in property, dividends, or cash. Stocks, bonds, and mortgages are securities.

**Seller's Option** — A special transaction on the Stock Exchange that gives the seller the right to deliver the stock or bond at any time within a specified period, ranging from not less than five business days to not more than 60 days.

**Shareholder or Stockholder** — One who legally owns one or more shares of the capital stock of a corporation. Shareholders often have a voice in the management of a business, sharing the risks of running a business and a business' profits.

**Shareholder**

**Short Covering** — Buying stock to return stock previously borrowed to make delivery on a short sale.

**Short Sale** — The sale for future delivery of securities, foreign exchange, or commodities not yet purchased or owned by the seller with the expectation that the price will drop in the interval and that it can be bought at a lower price later. (See Long.)

**Single Tax** — A concept first advanced in the 1800's by the "Physiocrats" of France, who argued that the only surplus arose from land, and therefore, only the land should be taxed; all other taxes interfered with the "natural order." Similar proposals, but suggesting other bases, have been advanced from time to time, with the latest perhaps being the "value added tax." (See Value Added Tax.)

**Sinking Fund** — Money set aside for the purpose of paying off an obligation that is to become due at some time in the future. Money regularly set aside by a company to redeem its bonds or preferred stock from time to time as specified in the indenture or charter.

**Socialism** — An economic and political philosophy whose adherants advocate government control or ownership and operation of the means of production and distribution, and the redistribution of income to achieve equality among all the members of society. Socialism can take a variety of forms, including Fabianism, Utopianism, and Communism.

**Solvency** — A term connoting the ability of a business to pay all of its debts out of the assets it holds. The condition that exists when liabilities other than those representing ownership amount to less than total assets. (See antonyms, Insolvency, and Bankruptcy.)

**Sovietism** — Of or pertaining to the Soviet Union, also used to describe the Soviet form of communism. Derived from "Soviet," the Russian term used for the various governing councils, from those at the village level to the Supreme Soviet. (See Bolshevism.)

**Special Bid** — A method of filling an order to buy a large block of stock on the floor of the Exchange. In a Special Bid, the bidder for the block of stock—a pension fund, for instance—will pay a special commission to the broker who represents him in making the purchase. The seller does not pay a commission.

**Specialist Block Purchase** — Purchase by the specialist for his own account of a large block of stock outside the regular market on the Exchange. Such purchases may be made only when the sale of the block could not be made in the regular market within a reasonable time and at reasonable prices, and when the purchase by the specialist would aid him in maintaining a fair and orderly market.

**Specialist Block Sale** — Opposite of the Specialist Block Purchase. Under exceptional circumstances, the specialist may sell a block of stock outside the regular market on the Exchange for his own account at a price above the prevailing market. The price is negotiated between the specialist and the broker for the buyer.

**Specie** — Full-bodied coin, and bullion, when it is used to "back" paper money or is represented by certificates convertible into gold or silver. Silver coins are the only specie presently in legal circulation in the United States.

**Speculation** — The purchase of anything that involves more than a minimum of risk with the intention of selling it quickly for more than it costs. Often applied to the buying and selling of stocks, commodities, or foreign exchange in the hope of making a profit because of changes in price. (See Investment.)

**Split** — The division of the outstanding shares of a corporation into a larger number of shares. A 3-for-1 split by a company with 1 million shares outstanding would result in 3 million shares outstanding. Splits usually occur in long established companies whose value per share makes it a "rich man's" stock. In a 3-1 split a $100 per share stock becomes about a $34 stock and attracts more buyers.

**Split System** — An economy in which a part of the tools of production and exchange are owned and operated by government, and the other part owned and operated by private citizens. Also called a mixed-economy.

**Stagflation** — An amalgam of *stagnation* and *inflation*. The condition when a nation's economy exhibits characteristics normally not observed at the same time—the inflation, shortages, and high interest rates typical of an economy at or near full production, coupled with the unemployment and sharply reduced business activity in major industries associated with a stagnant economy or one in recession.

**Standard of Living** — The amount and quality of goods and services, both necessities and luxuries, expressed in monetary terms needed to permit an individual family, or group to live at a certain economic level, either one they are accustomed to, or one to which they aspire.

**Stated Value or Declared Value** — No-par value stock whose value per share is designated by the board of directors of a corporation for capital account purposes.

**Stock Ahead** — Sometimes an investor who has entered an order to buy or sell stock at a certain price will see transactions at that price reported on the ticker tape while his own order has not been executed. The reason is that other buy and sell orders at the same price came in to the specialist ahead of his and had priority.

**Stock Certificate** — An engraved piece of paper that is evidence of ownership of stock in a corporation. Its loss may cause great inconvenience—even financial loss.

**Stock Dividend** — A dividend paid in securities rather than cash. The dividend may be additional shares of the issuing company, or in shares of another company (usually a subsidiary) held by the company.

Stock Exchange

**Stock Exchange** — An organized marketplace or clearinghouse where brokers buy and sell securities (mainly stock) for their customers, including individuals, banks, insurance companies, and private organizations and institutions.

**Stockholder of Record** — A stockholder whose name is registered on the books of the issuing corporation.

**Street Name** — Securities held in the name of a broker instead of his customer's name are said to be carried in a "street name." This occurs when the securities have been bought on margin or when the customer wishes the security to be held by the broker.

**Strike** — A temporary refusal by a group of employees to work. Employees strike to gain recognition of a union, to change working conditions, to get wage or benefit increases, and to support one side or the other on various political, economic, or social issues.

**Subsidiary** — A company controlled by another corporation called the parent company. The parent company wholly or partially owns the stock of the subsidiary. A subsidiary is, nevertheless, a legal corporate entity. (See Affiliate.)

**Subsidy** — Financial assistance or its equivalent extended to help provide a service that though deemed desirable or essential, is not economical from a profit or a self-supporting viewpoint. Can be either public or private, as subsidized company lunchrooms, but most often used to refer to direct monetary grants or payments by a government to an individual, business, or other group, or to another government.

**Supply and Demand** — See "Law of Supply and Demand."

**Surety** — A person or company, the guarantor, that guarantees the debt or performance of another in case of default. A written guaranty, surety bond, that protects a person against loss in case of default on a debt or performance of a contract and names the guarantor of the surety bond.

**Surplus** — The property of a business whose value is in addition to the amount paid in by the stockholders. Surplus is the property of the stockholders, even though it is withheld from them by management. The existence of surplus in a business usually makes the stock of that business rise in price so that it reflects the actual value of the business. (See antonym, Deficit.)

**Surtax** — A tax levied on top of or added to an existing tax.

**Syndicate** — A group of investment bankers who together underwrite a new issue of securities or a large block of an outstanding issue.

**Tariff** — A tax levied by a national government on imported goods but, rarely, on exported goods. This tax must be paid when the particular good crosses the nation's customs boundary. Tariffs are used by a national government to raise revenues, discourage the importation of certain goods, and as a discriminatory or retaliatory tool against a foreign country. Tariffs violate the precepts of free trade.

**Tax** — A monetary assessment on individuals and property legally determined, levied, and collected by government to support government functions for public purposes. A tax is a forced contribution of wealth for public or governmental needs.

**Tax Exempt Bonds** — The securities of states, cities, and other public authorities specified under Federal law, the interest on which is either wholly or partly exempt from Federal income taxes.

**Tax Foreclosure** — The seizure of property, due to the failure to pay taxes, by duly authorized government officials empowered to tax.

**Tax Penalty** — An extra charge or forfeiture of an amount of money because of the failure to pay taxes.

**Tax Receivership** — The function performed by a receiver appointed by a court or under the law upon non-payment of taxes.

**Tax Redemption** — The recovery of property by a settlement after the payment of delinquent taxes and tax penalties charged resulting from the delinquency.

**Tax Sale** — The sale of property, usually by public auction, for the non-payment of taxes. The public auction may be carried out by means of sealed or open bids.

**Taxable Income** — (Business) Income that remains after all costs other than profit have been subtracted. Profit, the cost of using the invested capital, is the last to be paid. The amount depends upon the ability of management and the willingness of the firm's customers to buy the company's products.
(Personal) Income that remains after deducting all legally non-taxable items.

**Tight Money** — A term used to describe the policy or course of action followed by a nation's monetary authority when it decides to restrict the growth of credit and to slow expansion of the nation's money supply to prevent or combat inflation. The United States Federal Reserve system implements a tight money policy by selling government securities to member banks, by increasing the legal reserves member banks must keep on hand, or by increasing the discount rate, which is the interest banks pay to borrow funds from the Federal Reserve, or a combination of all three. The first two reduce the amount of funds member banks have available to loan to individuals and businesses, and the third raises the cost of money to the banks. High interest rates result as businesses and individuals "bid" for available funds.

**Time Deposits** — A bank deposit that technically cannot be withdrawn without prior notice to the bank, often 30 days. In practice, this is rarely if ever enforced.

**To Move the Previous Question** — A formal motion at a meeting proposed to stop debate and vote immediately on a main motion. The previous question motion must have two-thirds vote to pass. If passed it does not mean the main motion has passed, but only that it will be voted upon by the assembly.

**Tools** — Tools are all things that aid human energy in the

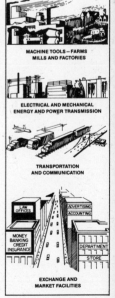

MACHINE TOOLS – FARMS MILLS AND FACTORIES

ELECTRICAL AND MECHANICAL ENERGY AND POWER TRANSMISSION

TRANSPORTATION AND COMMUNICATION

LAW OFFICES — ADVERTISING ACCOUNTING — MONEY BANKING CREDIT INSURANCE — DEPARTMENT STORE

EXCHANGE AND MARKET FACILITIES

**Tools**

process of changing the place, form, and characteristics of materials in the production and exchange of goods and services. Tools include such things as buildings, airplanes, office equipment, and machine tools.

**Totalitarianism** — A political system under which a relatively small group takes absolute control of government and are masters over the rest of the people. This mastery is held through the elimination of political opposition, by the control of the courts, and by terrorism, such as the use of secret police.

**Trade Association** — An association of businesses in a particular or related industry formed to promote their mutual interests through public affairs work; to collect and disseminate industry statistics; and, to provide a forum for member companies for the exchange of information and technological and managerial techniques and innovations in their industry. Examples of trade associations in the United States are the National Machine Tool Builder's Association and the National Association of Manufacturers.

**Transfer Agent** — A transfer agent keeps a record of the name of each registered shareowner, his or her address, the number of shares owned, and sees that certificates presented to his office for transfer are properly cancelled and new certificates issued in the name of the transferee.

**Treasury Bill** — A safe short-term security issued by the United States Treasury to raise cash. They are sold at public auction and usually mature in 91 or 182 days. Generally, treasury bills are purchased by large investors, such as commercial banks.

Treasury Note

**Treasury Note** — A safe security issued by the United States Treasury with a maturity date of one to five years. A treasury note is an intermediate-term security, falling between short-term treasury bills and the long-term government bonds that have maturity dates longer than five years.

**Treasury Stock** — Stock issued by a company but later reacquired. It may be held in the company's treasury indefinitely, reissued to the public or retired. Treasury stock receives no dividends and has no vote while held by the company.

**Trust** — A property interest created by a grantor or donor for the benefit of another called the beneficiary. This property is held and administered, but not owned, by a trustee in the interest of the beneficiary, usually under temporary or conditional terms such as until the beneficiary becomes of legal age.

**Trust Agreement** — A supplemental agreement that distributes the proceeds of a trust in a special way.

**Trust Deed** — A deed that establishes a trust, giving legal title of property to a trustee and stating his authority and obligations as administrator of the trust. It is sometimes used as a means to secure the lenders against loss and often used as a security resembling a mortgage.

**Trust Fund** — A fund of money or property that is legally set aside by a grantor or donor for the benefit of another person or organization called the beneficiary. A trust fund is administered by an individual such as a lawyer, or an organization, such as a bank, in the interest of the beneficiary.

**Trust Indenture** — An agreement whereby a third party holds the deed in trust as security for payment of a debt.

**Trustee** — An individual or company who holds the title to the property in a trust and administers it in the benefit and in the interest of the beneficiary. Banks and trust companies can act as trustees. Generally a trust company has a more permanent existence than the life of an individual, thus, the company may be combined with an individual trustee in a trust procedure.

**Turnover** — (Inventory) The number of times that a firm's inventory is completely cycled in a given time period. If per unit rates of return remain constant, higher turnover means greater profitability. The ratio of inventory to sales is a dynamic index number that gives an approximation of turnover, and also helps pinpoint "over-inventory" situations. (See Inventory.)

(Labor) The percentage of a firm's labor force that leaves the company for any reason in a given time period. When turnover exceeds a "normal" ratio, that is, turnover due to normal attrition, it tends to reduce operating efficiency and to increase costs.

**Underdeveloped Nation** — A nation whose people have a low per capita real income compared to the people of an industrial nation. The economies of underdeveloped nations are typically dominated by agriculture.

Also variously called "backward," "developing," "agricultural," or "third world" nations.

**Underemployment** — Situation in which workers, management or production tools are operating at an output rate below their productive capabilities or capacity. In economies with full employment policies, including state managed economies, underutilization of labor largely or entirely takes the form of underemployment rather than unemployment.

**Underutilization of Resources** — Condition that exists in an economy when it is not at or near full capacity and full employment and therefore, there is room for economic expansion without threat of inflation.

**Underwriter** — An individual or business concern that undertakes an insurance contract—an insurer or insurance company.

An individual or business concern, such as an investment bank, that underwrites security issues.

**Unearned Income** — Income that does not result directly from the production and exchange of goods and services. Actually, this is not unearned income unless it is in the form of a gift, since it involves extending some consideration in return for the income. It is usually in the form of interest, dividends, royalties, or the sale of some of the tools of the business.

**Union Shop** — A factory or other business establishment where all employees, except those on the management level, must join the labor union within a stated period of time after they are hired. (See antonym, Open Shop.)

**Unsecured Loan** — A loan not backed or secured by any collateral. It is simply made by the debtor signing a promissory note, which is held by the creditor until the debt is paid in full.

**Usury** — An interest rate or charge that is legally considered excessive and that, consequently, results in illegal profits for a creditor. In the United States, individual state laws define what is an excessive interest rate or charge in each respective state.

**Value** — The quantity of one thing that would be offered in exchange for another, usually expressed in terms of the standard medium of exchange; how much money a certain thing does or normally would bring in the market. Value is distinguished from cost and selling price in that cost and selling price are the records of actual transactions while value may or may not be.

**Value Added Tax** — A tax added at each step of production based upon the value added to the product or service at that stage. While it has been used as an *additional* tax in some nations many proponents argue that it should become the sole or "single tax" (See Single Tax) used to raise the funds necessary to pay for government activities. Reasoning is that all taxes are made possible by production, businesses are highly efficient tax collectors, and the rate of taxation could vary with the needs of the government. It would eliminate the Federal Income Tax and all its inequities, be virtually "cheatproof," and would cover the entire Gross National Product.

**Voting Right** — The stockholder's right to vote his stock in the affairs of his company. Most common shares have one vote each. The right to vote may be delegated by the stockholder to another person via a proxy.

**Voucher** — A receipt for a sum of money or a document showing a money payment of a debt. Vouchers are used to establish the accuracy of the entries in the books of account.

Voucher

**Warrant** — A written authorization or option to buy a security, generally a common stock, at a set price over an established period of time. Because a warrant is only an option to buy and not actual ownership of stock, it has no claim on either the equity or the profits of a company.

**Wealth** — Material objects that are useful or can be converted into useful form, relatively scarce, and transferable or appropriable. Usually expressed in terms of the money value of material objects that man can use and market.

**Welfare State** — A term applied to a state system under which large-scale governmental action is undertaken to furnish or guarantee such things as: (1) employment, (2) relief payments for those unemployed, (3) free or subsidized medical and dental care, (4) low cost housing, (5) low cost food, and (6) old age security. The costs are met through the taxes collected from the people, these taxes typically being at a progressive rate. (See Progressive Income Tax.)

There is a great difference of opinion as to the effects of the Welfare State on rights, freedom, production, willingness and incentive to work, and similar factors. Its supporters maintain: (1) that the people willingly will accept the necessary restrictions that the state must impose in exchange for what they get, and (2) that government is better able to plan and provide for the economic security of the individual than is the individual himself. Those who oppose the Welfare State maintain: (1) that when the need for the rewards of *personal* success are taken away, the people will not willingly work as well or produce as much, and (2) that to get the production that is absolutely essential to the welfare of the people, under the Welfare State, the government will be forced to resort to various forms of discipline and curb or eliminate most or all economic freedom.

**Wholesale** — The level of business distribution at which a merchant purchases goods, normally in quantity, from producers primarily for resale to retail merchants. In effect, the wholesaler is a middleman acting as the intermediary between the producer and the retailer who sells the goods to the ultimate consumer. (See Middleman and Retail.)

**Wholesale Price Index** — A statistical, monthly, numerical index used to measure changes in wholesale prices for such commodities as machinery, oil, and food. The Index is issued by the United States Bureau of Labor Statistics. Current wholesale prices are expressed as a percentage of averages for the comparable part of a given prior year called the "base period." The Wholesale Price Index is a good indicator of the effects of inflation on the economy because retail prices increase or decrease roughly in line with changes in wholesale prices, but with some lag.

**Without Recourse** — Words used in endorsing a note or other negotiable instrument indicating that the future holder is not to look to the endorser in case of non-payment. Also, in a sales contract, an agreement that the buyer of some good or service accepts all risks pertaining to a transaction and relinquishes any rights of recourse.

**Working Capital** — The total current assets, less the total current liabilities, that can be used in conducting the operations of a business. It must be distinguished from fixed capital, which is the capital invested in fixed assets, such as buildings.

**Working Control** — Theoretically, ownership of 51 per cent of a company's voting stock is necessary to exercise control. In practice—particularly in case of a large corporation—effective control sometimes can be exerted through a much smaller percentage.

**Write-Off** — Removing an uncollectable debt or other worthless assets from the account books of a company by reducing it to zero and entering it as a loss or bad debt.

**Xerox** — Trade name of the manufacturer of Xerox machines employed for the photocopying of printed material. The desired image is deposited on each copy by a dry powder that is fused onto ordinary bond paper by a process called xerography.

**Yield** — The annual return on a financial investment expressed as a percentage of its cost: for example, a $1,000 investment in common stocks that pays $50 in annual dividends yields 5%.

**Yield to Maturity** — A measure of the rate of return expressed in a percentage that will be obtained on an investment if the investment is held to maturity. It is based on a formula that takes into consideration the price paid for the investment, the price at maturity, the term or number of years to maturity, and the annual rate of interest.

**Zero** — The concept of the cipher (Arabian, sifer, "nothing") was introduced about 200 B.C. in the Middle East. With zero representing the metaphoric nothing or naught, the Arabic numeral system became much simpler to use than the cumbersome and inefficient Roman numeral system. The zero or comparable symbol is essential to positional notation or indication of value—units, tens, hundreds, thousands, etc.—by virtue of position in relation to the decimal place.

**Zoning** — The legal enactment of ordinances by a public body to regulate the character and the intensity of the use of property in the public interest. For example, a city council may pass zoning ordinances that reserve one section of the city for the building of single-family houses only and another section of the city for the construction of factories.